11+
English
Success

in the
11+ tests

Anne Rooney, Val Mitchell, Sally Moon

Contents

Introduction	About the 11+ tests	4
	Five steps to success	5
	The 11+ English tests	6
1 Find out what you know	How this book will help you	8
	Where you are now	9
	Taking the tests	10
	Marking the tests	11
2 Plan your practice	Summarising the tests	12
	Understanding the grids	13
	Reading grid 1	14
	Writing grids	15
	Dictation and spelling grids 1	17
3 Improve your skills	*Reading*	
Comprehension	Introducing comprehension	18
	Skimming and scanning text	20
	Finding information	22
	Deduction and inference	26
	Organisation of text	28
	How writers use language	30
	Writer's viewpoint	32
	Traditional and social context	34
Grammar	*Introducing grammar*	*36*
	Parts of speech	38
	Figurative language	40
	Starting sentences	42
	Agreement in sentences	44
Punctuation	*Introducing punctuation*	*46*
	Basic punctuation	48
	More about punctuation	50
Spelling	*Introducing spelling*	*52*
	Plurals and spelling rules	54
	Doubling letters	56
	Prefixes and suffixes	58
	Tricky spellings	60

Writing

Fiction, plays and poetry	*Introducing fiction, plays, and poetry*	62
	Writing stories	64
	Writing plays	66
	Writing poems	67
Non-fiction	*Introducing non-fiction writing*	68
	Writing discussion texts	69
	Writing explanatory texts	70
	Instructional and procedural texts	71
	Non-chronological reports	72
	Persuasive writing	73
	Recount texts	74
	Letter writing	75

English essentials

Different styles of fiction writing	76
Glossary	78

4 Test for success

The next steps	82
Reading grid 2	83
Dictation and spelling grids 2	84
Reaching your destination	85

5 Show what you can do

Preparing for the 11+ tests	86
Interview techniques	88
After the tests	90

Test answers

Improve your skills *answers*	91
Reading test 1 *answers*	95
Reading test 2 *answers*	96

Practice tests

Pull-out section	
Reading test 1	1
Reading test 2	7
Dictation and spelling tests 1	14
Dictation and spelling tests 2	15
Writing tasks	16

About the 11+ tests

Introduction

The 11+ tests are used by schools to find out about your thinking and learning skills and how you apply these to comprehension (understanding), writing, maths and problem solving.

You will be asked to take a selection of tests that could include some or all of the subjects listed on this page. There are a number of standardised tests schools can use, although some local authorities and schools write their own tests. This book guides you through the question styles, formats and levels of difficulty in the standardised tests, as well as providing examples of other question types that frequently occur.

Schools will often give you an interview in addition to the tests so that they can find out more about you. They may also set a problem-solving task.

Subjects set in the 11+ tests

English
The English paper will consist of a reading test and may also contain a separate writing task. There is no standardised form of writing task and schools often create their own. The papers are generally divided in the following ways.

Reading
- Comprehension
- Grammar
- Punctuation
- Spelling

Writing

Essential research
- Find out as much information as possible about your selected schools well in advance.
- You can find information on dates and entrance exams for state grammar schools on your local authority website or the school website.
- Individual schools include information in their prospectuses and additional information is often available on the school websites or at open days.
- Closing dates for applications vary, so you should check these well in advance.

Maths
The Maths paper will consist of a written test and probably a mental maths test in which the questions are read out to you. Calculators are not allowed in either test. Schools often write their own mental maths tests. The papers generally test the following skills.

Main test
- Numbers and their properties
- Calculations (including algebra)
- Fractions, decimals and percentages
- Working with charts and data
- Shape and space
- Measuring
- Data handling

Mental maths test

Verbal reasoning
Verbal reasoning tests ask you to solve puzzles and problems that involve letters, words and numbers and the connections between them.

Non-verbal reasoning
Non-verbal reasoning tests ask you to solve puzzles and problems that involve visual patterns or sequences and their connections.

Introduction

Five steps to success

11+ English Success is designed to help you prepare for the 11+ English paper in **five simple steps** so that you can take the tests with confidence.

The colour-coded sections in this guide split up the process, making it easy to follow.

1 Test — Find out what you know

Take Test 1 in the centre of the book and mark your answers. This will show what you already know and where you need to do more work.

2 Track — Plan your practice

Fill in the grids to target the specific skills you want to develop. This will help you to plan your work and decide how much time you need to set aside.

3 Teach — Improve your skills

Work through the Skills pages indicated by your grids and test yourself with the questions at the end of each section. All the answers are clearly explained to help you understand where you have gone wrong if you make any mistakes. Colour in the progress chart.

4 Test — Test for success

Take Test 2 in the centre of the book and mark your scores on the second set of grids to find out how you have improved.

Missed a few skills? Don't worry, just go back through any of the Skills pages you need to work on…

You can now move on to a full 11+ test, fully prepared. Look at the list of papers available on the inside front cover to see which is most suitable for you.

5 Present — Show what you can do

Practise your presentation skills using the interview tips and techniques on pages 88–89. If you are asked for an interview at the school you have chosen, this is your chance to shine.

Introduction

The 11+ English tests are designed to test your basic knowledge of English and also to test how well you can analyse and interpret texts.

You are likely to have two tests to do: one to find out about your **reading** skills and one to find out about your **writing** skills. The Reading test can include the following sections (although they may not be labelled).

Reading test

Comprehension

The skills covered

This section will test that you can understand the main points of a text you are given.

What you will have to do

You will be asked questions to see if you can…

- find specific information
- look for clues that help explain things
- comment on how the text is organised
- pick out and explain words and phrases
- give an opinion about the purpose of a text
- identify the time or place in which a text is set.

Grammar

The skills covered

The English Grammar section will test your understanding of how sentences and paragraphs can be linked and joined in different ways to create different effects.

What you will have to do

You will be asked questions to see if you can…

- identify and name parts of speech
- match verbs and tenses (make them agree)
- spot a range of language techniques and understand how they make the writing more interesting.

Punctuation

The skills covered

This section will test your understanding of how punctuation works to make a text that is easy to read.

What you will have to do

You will be asked to see whether you can…

- use capital letters and full stops in a range of ways
- use exclamation marks and question marks correctly
- use apostrophes for contractions and belonging
- use commas to create lists and separate clauses
- punctuate direct speech using inverted commas and the correct layout
- show an understanding of colons and semi-colons.

Spelling

The skills covered

This section will test how well you can follow the basic principles of spelling.

What you will have to do

You will be asked to see if you can…

- follow key rules for changing words from singular to plural
- add prefixes and suffixes correctly
- spell common irregular words
- remember words that have different meanings and spellings but the same sound.

Writing task

The skills covered

Most schools also ask you to complete a writing task. These tasks are set by individual schools. The writing task may either be included in the same test as the reading skills or given as a completely separate test. The writing task is included so that you can show the school that you can create interesting texts that demonstrate all of your writing skills.

What you will have to do

You will be given a writing brief that explains the type of text you need to write. It could be fiction or non-fiction.

INTERVIEWS

Schools often make their final selection by interviewing the candidates. This is where you get a chance to show your potential to be a good member of the school, and to find out whether this is the right place for you. Find out about more about interview techniques on pages 88–89.

SATs practice

The English SATs that you take at the end of Year 6 also contains reading and writing assessments, so all the skills you learn in this book will help you to tackle those as well. The question types are similar and test the same skills.

Once you have mastered these important skills you will find that they help you in communicating with others, both at school and in the world outside.

The **Comprehension** and **Grammar** sections in the book (pages 18–45) will help you in…

- understanding the meaning of texts and how to pick out key words and phrases within them for the SATs Reading paper
- improving your creative writing for the SATs short and long writing tasks with an increased awareness of the range of sentence structures you can use and the creative language needed to convey meaning within them.

The **Punctuation** and **Spelling** sections (pages 46–61) will help you with the spelling tests and the writing tasks at SATs in Year 6.

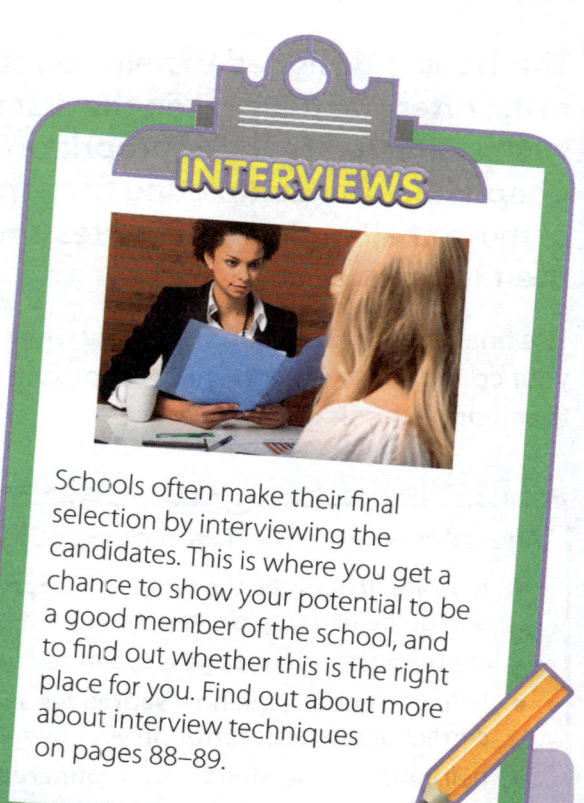

The **Writing** and **English essentials** sections (pages 62–77) will help you to…

- identify the writing genres you will need to be familiar with in the SATs writing tasks
- plan and structure your work as well as build tension and excitement in the long SATs writing task
- craft sentences and work quickly to create short texts with impact for the short SATs writing task.

Try out some of the writing tasks at the end of the pull-out test booklet to improve your writing skills further.

The **Glossary** (pages 78–81) will help you to understand the technical vocabulary in the SATs English papers. It contains important language vocabulary you will have been taught in school and will be expected to know in these assessments. The terms are highlighted in bold.

1 Find out what you know

How this book will help you

This book is designed to help you succeed in your 11+ English tests. After you have taken the first set of Practice tests, you will be directed to the appropriate *Improve your skills* pages in Chapter 3. After completing these pages, use the second set of more challenging Practice tests to check you are ready for the 11+ tests.

The final chapter in the book, *5 Show what you can do*, will help you to build your confidence as the 11+ tests approach and prepare you for the interview that many schools give.

Understanding the skills

After taking the first set of Practice tests, Chapter 3 *Improve your skills* will…

- help you to identify the types of **comprehension** questions that you find difficult and guide you step by step through the strategies that will help you with them
- show you how **language** is organised to make texts easy to understand
- help you understand how **sentences** and **paragraphs** work so that you can correct grammatical errors in your own and other people's work
- help you to understand how to **punctuate sentences** so that they are easy to read
- show you how to remember the important **English spelling rules** and alert you to the exceptions to these rules
- explain the **types of writing style and organisation** expected in fiction and non-fiction writing.

Practising the skills

To help you practise these skills as you work through the book, you will find…

- example questions and a short test in each section, providing extra practice
- 'Try it out' activities to build your skills
- opportunities to complete short and long writing tasks
- a straightforward marking grid that helps you identify and improve the key skills of effective writing
- a glossary of words that occur frequently in the tests.

Preparing for the tests

When your practice is complete, Chapter *5 Show what you can do* on pages 86–89 can help you to relax and prepare yourself in the final week. It contains…

- a range of activities to do with your parents and friends to help you become more familiar with the skills you have learned in comprehension, grammar and spelling
- a 'countdown' list to help you get ready
- interview advice on how to dress, relax and communicate
- information about what happens after you get your 11+ test results.

1 Find out what you know

Where you are now

Before you begin your 11+ practice, you need to work out how much you already know. As well as using this book, you may find it helpful to ask your school or your tutor about the skills you need to work on. The Internet is another useful source of information.

School
Your class teachers will have given you a number of tests during your time at school and they can give you helpful feedback about your progress in reading and writing.

Reading age
- There are several different reading tests that you may have taken. Some of these are to test your ability to understand vocabulary; some are to test your reading and comprehension skills. Don't be afraid to ask which test or tests you have taken.
- The school should have a record of your reading age in years and months and this can be compared to your actual age. The school may also have recorded a 'standardised' score (a score that is reliable because of the number of people who have taken the test before you), which compares your results to those of other children who are the same age as you.
- Ideally, your reading age should be at least one year ahead of your actual age before taking the 11+ tests.

Spelling age
- Some schools test spelling and give spelling ages, similar to the reading tests. These spelling ages can be compared with your actual age.
- Ideally, your spelling age should be at least one year ahead of your actual age.
- You can test your own spelling skills using the tests in this book and by trying out simple exercises available on the Internet.
- Learn 'the awful speller's alphabet' to help you with some difficult words.

All right	**J**udge	**S**uccess
Beautiful	**K**nowledge	**T**omorrow
Committee	**L**ibrary	**U**ntil
Definite	**M**edicine	**V**egetable
Eighth	**N**ecessary	**W**ednesday
February	**O**urs	**X**ylophone
Gorgeous	**P**arliament	**Y**ours
Hamster	**Q**uestionnaire	**Z**ebra
Independent	**R**eceive	

SATs (the Statutory Assessment Tests)
- You will have taken one in Year 2 and will take another at the end of Year 6.
- The average Level attained at Year 2 is Level 2; the average Level attained at Year 6 is Level 4.
- Your school may predict the level you will reach in English at the end of each Key Stage and you can ask for these records.

Teacher's assessment
Teachers assess your progress during the year in English. This assessment is often scored in thirds of a Level: 2c, 2b, 2a; 3c, 3b, 3a; 4c, 4b, 4a; 5c, 5b, 5a. An 'a' score is the highest in each Level.

Tutors
If you are using an independent tutor or tuition school, they will have similar information to your own school. They may also have data on your Non-verbal reasoning and Verbal reasoning abilities.

Taking the tests

1 Find out what you know

Now you are ready to take the Practice tests, it is important to make sure you have the right conditions to get an accurate result.

These Practice tests (located in the pull-out booklet) will help you to identify the areas you will need to target for further practice.

Timing
It is better to do the tests in two mornings at a weekend when you are at your best, rather than after school when you have had a long day.

Allow the following times for each test plus at least half an hour to get everything organised.

Day 1
Reading test 1: 45 minutes
Dictation test 1: about 15 minutes.

Day 2
Writing task 1: 45 minutes
Spelling test 1: about 15 minutes.

Equipment
You should have the following items assembled before you begin:
- pen
- pencil
- eraser
- pencil sharpener
- ruler
- timer (this can be the timer on an oven or an alarm clock)
- analogue watch/clock (as this will help you to see how much time you've got left)
- paper (for jotting ideas; your start and finish times; Dictation, Writing and Spelling tests).

Surroundings
You should use a clear table or desk so that you can set out the materials you will be using.

Make sure the area is quiet and without any distractions.

You will need to make sure somebody is available to help you with the Spelling and Dictation tests. These will need to be read aloud to you so that you can write your answers down.

Question types
Multiple-choice
If you are taking a 'standardised' 11+ Reading test, you can expect this to be in a multiple-choice format set out in different styles by section. You are also likely to have a separate booklet to mark your answers in.

Comprehension
After reading a passage, the grammar questions typically ask you to choose from a list of options provided. You will find a lot of these in the Reading tests in this book to help you become familiar with this type of question. Always complete them in **exactly** the way you are instructed.

Grammar, punctuation and spelling
Grammar, punctuation and spelling questions in the standardised tests are typically set out with the letter options underneath words, or groups of words, in sentences. There are several examples of these question types in the Reading tests in this book.

Written format
When local authorities, schools and examination boards set their own papers, some or all of the questions are likely to be in a written format. For these questions, you will not be given any options to choose from. Some of the questions require one-word answers, others a phrase, and a third type will require you to give a longer response with reference to the text.

TIPS FOR SUCCESS
- Read each question twice.
- Check carefully what you are being asked to look for.
- Don't guess any answers even if you are short of time. These tests are to help you find out areas where you need practice.

1 Find out what you know

Once you have completed the Practice tests in the pull-out booklet, you will be ready to mark them. Do this by following the stages below.

Marking

Reading test

- Go to the *Answers* on page 95. Score your completed paper by filling in the blank boxes in the 'Mark column'. There is one mark allowed for each complete question – **there are no half marks**.
- Now turn to *Reading grid 1* on page 14.
- Transfer your marks to the 'Mark*' column. 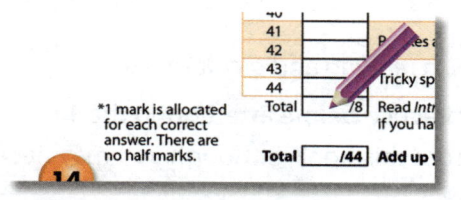
- Add up the total for each section.
- Add up the total for all the sections in the final box at the end of the Reading grid.
- Work out the percentage as directed in the Summary box on page 12.

Dictation test

- Go to *Dictation grid 1* on page 17 and compare it against your completed Dictation test. Put a line through the box for each word or punctuation mark you have spelt or included **correctly** (you must have capital letters in the correct places too). 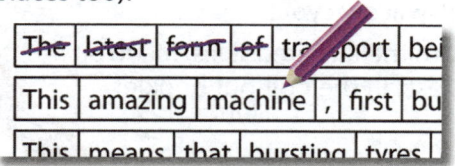
- Add up the number of **blank** boxes (these are the words and punctuation marks that you have omitted or are **incorrect**)
- Subtract this total from 100. For example, if you have 7 errors (blanks), subtract this number from 100 to give you a final score of 93.
- Transfer this final number to the Summary box on page 12. This is the percentage mark.

Writing task

- Go to the *Writing grid* on page 15 if you have produced a fiction text or page 16 for a non-fiction text. Photocopy the grid so that you can use it again later.
- Work with an adult to go through the grid one section at a time. Refer to the Glossary on pages 78–81 for any difficult words.
- Read the text for each Level and then decide which text most closely applies to your piece of writing.
- Once you have decided the Level that applies to you, colour the related block in the Level column orange.
- Transfer your Levels for each section to the Summary boxes on page 12.

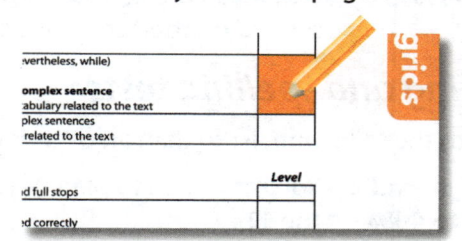

Spelling tests

- Go to the *Spelling grid 1* on page 17 and compare it with your completed Spelling tests. Tick each word you have spelt **correctly**.
- Add up the number of ticks to give your total.
- Work out the percentage as directed in the Summary box on page 12.

11

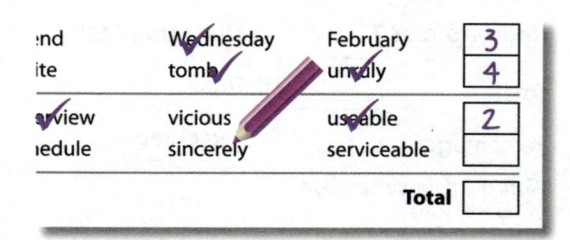

2 Plan your practice

Summarising the tests

Now that you have all your results from the first Practice tests, you can begin to plan your time to work on the skills you may need to practise.

Understanding the summary boxes

The Summary boxes at the bottom of this page will help you to build an overview of the key areas you will need to concentrate on in your 11+ practice. You should also view your results in relation to the information you found out from your research on page 9, 'Where you are now'.

Reading and dictation tests

Refer to the list below to get an overview of your abilities in *reading* and *dictation*.

Up to 50%	You may need to plan 9–12 months of practice before attempting the 11+.
51–60%	Feel encouraged that you will benefit from this book, although you may need to work through most of the skills pages.
61–80%	You have many skills that will help you in your 11+ tests already and will benefit from the support this book will give you.
81–100%	When you are confident in working with the targeted skills, move on to the second (harder) set of Practice tests in the pull-out booklet.

Writing and spelling tests

Refer to the following list to gain an overview of your abilities in *writing* and *spelling*.

Mostly Level 2 or up to 40%	You may need to plan 9–12 months of practice before attempting the 11+.
Mostly Level 3 or 41–50%	Feel encouraged that you will benefit from this book, although you may need to work through most of the skills pages.
Mostly Level 4 or 51–70%	You have many skills that will help you in your 11+ tests already and will benefit from the support this book will give you.
Mostly Level 5 or 71–100%	When you are confident in working with the targeted skills, move on to the second (harder) set of Practice tests in the pull-out booklet.

Summary boxes

Reading test 1

Total [ ]
Percentage [ ]

Work out your percentage using this sum

$\frac{\text{Total}}{44} \times 100 =$

Dictation test 1

Total [ ]
Percentage [ ]

Writing task 1

Section	Level
Grammar	[ ]
Punctuation	[ ]
Spelling	[ ]
Text structure	[ ]

Spelling test 1

Total [ ]
Percentage [ ]

Work out your percentage using this sum

$\frac{\text{Total}}{50} \times 100 =$

2 Plan your practice

Understanding the grids

The Reading grid

Reading grid 1 on page 14 (where you have marked your scores for Reading test 1) is an essential tool in planning your 11+ practice.

Turn to the grid and look at the 'To do' column. You will see that questions are grouped into blocks.

- Colour the blocks in **green** where you have answered **all** the questions **right**.
- Colour the blocks in **red** where you have answered **some or all** of the questions **wrong**.

Red sections

Look at the sections (Comprehension, Grammar, Punctuation and Spelling) where you have coloured blocks in red. Begin by reading the relevant Introductions to these sections in Chapter *3 Improve your skills* (the page numbers are written next to the headings). For example, if you have coloured 'Skimming and scanning text' in red, then you should begin by reading *'Introducing comprehension'* on page 20. Now work through the rest of the section in *3 Improve your skills* to complete the skills you marked in red earlier:

- Read through the text.
- Have a go at the 'Try it out' activities.
- Complete the questions at the end (and check your answers on pages 91–94).
- When you have finished the skill, colour in the 'Try it out' and 'Test yourself' boxes on Reading grid 1.

Make a note of any questions you found difficult so that you can go back to these pages again before you take the 11+ test.

Green sections

If you have coloured any blocks in green, you have already mastered some of the easier skills needed in these sections, so you may not want to go through them as thoroughly. However, skimming quickly through the pages and trying out some activities will provide you with some tips to help you to speed up your test technique and tackle more difficult questions.

Working through the questions on these pages will also help to build your confidence in areas that you enjoy.

The Writing grids

The Writing grids provide a helpful tool in the next step of your writing practice.

These grids are designed to give you a broad idea of your current abilities. To get the best picture of your progress in writing it is also helpful to look at any information you have received from your school (after your research on page 9) to see if your findings match up.

Look at each section in your completed Writing grid (Grammar, Punctuation, Spelling and Text structure) and review the Levels you have given yourself against the list below.

- **Level 2:** You should work through this whole section in the book, even if you have answered some of the questions correctly in the Reading test.
- **Level 3:** We recommend that you work through this whole section in the book. If you feel confident with the skill, just answer the questions at the end of the section to test your knowledge.
- **Level 4:** We recommend answering the questions in the section to practise your skills.
- **Level 5:** You may wish to work through some questions to build confidence in the skills.

If you are at Level 4 or below, we also recommend working through the genre page relating to the writing exercise you have just completed. These are on pages 64–75 (see contents page for a full list). You should also work through other pages in this section where you lack confidence.

Go to page 17 for information about how to understand your Dictation and Spelling test results.

Example of Reading grid, marked with colour blocks

Reading grid 1

2 Plan your practice

Follow the instructions on page 11 to fill in this grid and page 13 for instructions for use.

Comprehension

Question	Mark*	Skill	Page	To do	Try it out	Test yourself
1		Skimming and scanning text	20			
2						
3		Finding information	22			
4						
5						
6						
7		Deduction and inference	26			
8						
9						
10		Organisation of text	28			
11						
12						
13						
14		How writers use language	30			
15						
16		Writer's viewpoint	32			
17						
18		Traditional and social context	34			
19						
Total	/19	Read 'Introducing comprehension' first on pages 18–19 if you have missed any Skills in the Comprehension section.				

Grammar

Question	Mark*	Skill	Page	To do	Try it out	Test yourself
20		Parts of speech	38			
21						
22						
23		Figurative language	40			
24						
25		Starting sentences	42			
26						
27		Agreement in sentences	44			
28						
29						
30						
Total	/11	Read 'Introducing grammar' first on pages 36–37 if you have missed any Skills in the Grammar section.				

Punctuation

Question	Mark*	Skill	Page	To do	Try it out	Test yourself
31		Basic punctuation	48			
32						
33						
34		More about punctuation	50			
35						
36						
Total	/6	Read 'Introducing punctuation' first on pages 46–47 if you have missed any Skills in the Punctuation section.				

Spelling

Question	Mark*	Skill	Page	To do	Try it out	Test yourself
37		Plurals and spelling rules	54			
38						
39		Doubling letters	56			
40						
41		Prefixes and suffixes	58			
42						
43		Tricky spellings	60			
44						
Total	/8	Read 'Introducing spelling' first on pages 52–53 if you have missed any Skills in the Spelling section.				

*1 mark is allocated for each correct answer. There are no half marks.

Total /44 Add up your total for your Reading test here.

2 Plan your practice

Fiction
Follow the instructions on page 11 to mark these grids and page 13 to fill in the Level assignments.

Language features

Grammar *see pages 36–45*   **Level**

Level 2	simple **connectives** (and, but, so, then)
Level 3	**connectives** (but, when, also, because, so, if)
	subjects and **verbs** generally agree
	simple **noun** phrases and **adverbs**
Level 4	**connectives** (meanwhile, although, nevertheless, while)
	subjects and **verbs** agree
	contains **simple sentences** and one **complex sentence**
	some imaginative vocabulary or vocabulary related to the text
Level 5	contains a mixture of **simple** and **complex sentences**
	imaginative vocabulary or vocabulary related to the text

Punctuation *see pages 46–51*   **Level**

Level 2	some **sentences** with **capital letters** and **full stops**
Level 3	some **speech marks**
	at least half of all **sentences** punctuated correctly
Level 4	**speech marks** used correctly with a new speaker starting on a new line
	sentences punctuated correctly
Level 5	a range of **punctuation** (**brackets**, **dashes**, ellipses, **colons**) for impact and interest

Spelling *see pages 52–61*   **Level**

Level 2	simple constant **vowel** clusters (CVC) and common irregular words spelt correctly (first 200 word list)
Level 3	words spelt correctly as they are sounded
	most common irregular words spelt correctly
	standard beginnings and endings, e.g. Once upon a time… spelt correctly
Level 4	most words spelt correctly including past and present **tense**, time, **prepositions**
Level 5	spelling correct including **suffixes, prefixes** and more complex content words

Text structure   **Level**

Level 2	an opening **sentence**
	two or more events in order
	two or more characters
Level 3	a clear opening
	a sensible order of events and a simple ending
	information about the characters (such as their past, likes and dislikes, personality)
	a description of a setting that uses descriptive words to locate it clearly
Level 4	an effective opening that makes the reader want to continue
	a clear beginning and an organised middle and ending
	a variety of characters with differing features that work together in a clear way
	a description of a setting that uses descriptive words to make it appear real
Level 5	an effective opening building interest and creating impact
	well-structured **paragraphs** sympathetic to the content
	a balance of description, storyline and speech
	use of flashbacks and two events happening at the same time
	information about the characters (such as their past, likes and dislikes, personality)
	a description of a setting conveying the atmosphere and its effect on the characters

2 Plan your practice

Non-fiction

Follow the instructions on page 11 to mark these grids and page 13 to fill in the Level assignments.

Language features

Grammar see pages 36–45 — **Level**

Level 2	simple **connectives** (and, but, so, then)
Level 3	**connectives** (but, when, also, because, so, if)
	subjects and **verbs** generally agree
	simple **noun** phrases and **adverbs**
Level 4	**connectives** (whereas, furthermore, in addition)
	subjects and **verbs** agree
	contains **simple sentences** and one **complex sentence**
	some technical vocabulary or vocabulary related to the subject
Level 5	contains a mixture of **simple** and **complex sentences**
	technical vocabulary or vocabulary related to the subject

Punctuation see pages 46–51 — **Level**

Level 2	some **sentences** with **capital letters** and **full stops**
Level 3	some **speech marks**
	at least half of all **sentences** punctuated correctly
Level 4	**speech marks** used correctly with a new speaker starting on a new line
	sentences punctuated correctly
Level 5	a range of **punctuation** (**brackets**, **dashes**, ellipses, **colons**) for impact and interest

Spelling see pages 52–61 — **Level**

Level 2	simple constant **vowel** clusters (CVC) and common irregular words spelt correctly (first 200 word list)
Level 3	words spelt correctly as they are sounded
	most common irregular words spelt correctly
Level 4	standard vocabulary linked to non-fiction structure, e.g. advert for 'sale' or 'reduction'
	most words spelt correctly including past and present **tense**, time, **prepositions**
Level 5	spelling correct including **suffixes, prefixes** and technical words

Text structure — **Level**

Level 2	a heading and/or introduction, basic address elements in letters
	some information set out in the correct order
	a section that relates to a heading
Level 3	mostly correct structure for the non-fiction type (see pages 69–75)
	similar pieces of information grouped together in sections
	sections all link to their headings
Level 4	correct structure for the non-fiction type (see pages 69–75)
	text grouped together in **paragraphs** and headings (appropriate to text type) in a logical order
	a breakdown of heading levels (appropriate to text type)
Level 5	purpose and **context** of the text clear
	text grouped in a thoughtful way supported by relevant argument and detail
	headings laid out clearly and imaginatively (appropriate to text type)
	style of writing adapted to the text type: personal or formal

Writing grids

2 Plan your practice

Dictation grid 1

Follow the instructions on page 11 to mark this grid.

| What | 's | Floating | Over | London | ? |

| The | latest | form | of | transport | being | considered | for | our | inner | cities | is | the | hovercraft | . |

| This | amazing | machine | , | first | built | in | the | 1950s | , | can | travel | over | different | surfaces | . |

| This | means | that | bursting | tyres | on | potholes | will | be | a | thing | of | the | past | . |

| The | London | Mayor | is | very | keen | on | this | idea | and | has | already | planned | a |

| competition | to | find | the | best | logo | to | decorate | the | hover | fleet | . | The | race | is | on | . |

| " | Send | us | your | most | inventive | plans | , | " | urges | the | scheme | 's | new | Project | Manager | . |

The Dictation test can help you to identify problems in your own creative writing. If there are a lot of omissions, you may find that you often think of a word but leave it out because you have difficulty in writing it down.

Look carefully at the errors in your test and see if you have left words out, missed punctuation marks or put in additional words.

The test will also give you practice in proof-reading your own work and help you to improve this.

If you miss punctuation, this could highlight a problem with your understanding of sentence structure. Revising parts of speech and sentence construction (see pages 38–39 and 42–45) will help to improve this.

Spelling grid 1

Follow the instructions on page 11 to mark this grid.

A	pad	ten	fig	got	but	
	any	you	why	talk	true	
B	trot	grim	rush	them	silk	
	view	bird	each	early	final	
C	clear	slice	liar	mouse	weave	
	bright	should	awful	busy	juice	
D	island	once	friend	Wednesday	February	
	feather	exciting	quite	tomb	unruly	
E	referred	questionnaire	interview	vicious	useable	
	cemetery	secretary	schedule	sincerely	serviceable	
					Total	

Look carefully at the types of word you have spelt incorrectly in the test. If you found a lot of errors in parts A and B of the test, you may benefit from revising your phonics. Make sure you check internal vowels as well as the beginning and ending letters or blends.

If you found a lot of errors in parts C and D you would benefit from revising the Spelling section of this book (see pages 52–61).

If you had difficulty with the second lines of each part and found part E challenging, it is time to practise the exercises in the Spelling sections to find ways to help you get these irregular word spellings into your long-term memory.

Introducing comprehension

3 Improve your skills: Reading

'Comprehension' means 'understanding'. A comprehension test gives you the chance to show you have understood a piece of writing.

Comprehension questions test your **understanding** of what the text says, its aims or purpose, its point of view and how it gets information across. The questions also test whether you understand when and where the events in the text take place.

What to expect

Comprehension passages can be any type of writing at all. They may be stories, plays or poems, or they may be from informative texts such as articles, adverts, descriptions, journals or instructions.

There may be different types of questions in a comprehension test. Some are multiple-choice questions: you have to pick the right answer. For other questions, you may need to write your own answer, either in a few words or whole **sentences**. Make sure you know what you have to do before you start answering.

Comprehension exercises test your understanding of what the text says literally – what it tells you directly – and what it implies or suggests. You will sometimes need to 'read between the lines' to look for clues.

Comprehension skills

When you approach a comprehension exercise, you will need to work out…

- *who* or *what* the text is about
- *when* and *where* it relates to or takes place (if it's a story)
- *why* the events happen or *why* the writer has written the information
- *whose* 'voice' the text presents.

Look at the story extract then read through the following questions and explanations.

1. In the test, you will be expected to be able to answer all of the following question types.
   - *Who* is 'Finding a bone' about?

     It's about Drew and Martin, who are brothers. You can find this information in the text. 'Drew…hated his little brother rushing into his room.'

Finding a bone

'Drew! Look what I've got!'

Martin bounced onto Drew's bed. Drew scowled at him. He hated his little brother rushing into his room without knocking. Drew looked at what Martin held in his hand.

'Cool! A bone. Where did you get it?'

'Outside. I was playing with my lorries. It was in the dirt. Is it from a person?'

'Looks like a bone from a dog's tail. Let's clean the mud off.'

They scrubbed the bone under the tap with the nail brush.

'It's definitely a tail bone,' Drew said. But he wasn't sure.

Soldier Boy, by Anne Rooney

Comprehension

- *What* is it about?

  It's about what happened when Martin found a bone while playing with his lorries. The title gives you a clue. In a factual piece of writing, the first sentence often tells you what the text is about.

- *When* and *where* does it take place?

  This passage takes place in Drew's bedroom (because Martin bounced onto Drew's bed). We can't tell exactly when, but it's in the daytime as Martin has been playing outside.

- *Why* has Drew come into Martin's room?

  He has come in to show Drew the bone.
  We can't yet tell where this story is going to go, or why the bone is important.

- *Whose* voice tells the story?

  We are not told anything about the **narrator** (the voice telling the story), but we can tell that it is not a character in the story.

What you will learn

In this section you will learn these comprehension topics…
- skimming and scanning text
- finding information
- deduction and inference
- organisation of the text
- writer's use of language
- writer's viewpoint
- traditional and social context.

2 You are very likely to be asked questions that give you a choice of answer. You should consider all the answers carefully as the obvious choice is not always correct. Always check back against the text before making your final choice.

- Why do Drew and Martin scrub the bone under the tap?

  A because it is unhygienic

  B to clean the mud off so that they can see it properly

  C so that they don't get into trouble for playing with something dirty

  D so that they can keep it

  E so that they can call the police if it is a human bone.

  This question is not answered directly in the text, so you have to work out why they wash the bone. They are not sure what type of bone it is. They wash the bone, then Drew says he knows it is a dog's tail bone. You can tell from this that they wash the bone so that they can see it more clearly (answer B).

TIPS FOR SUCCESS

Tackling comprehension

- Understanding starts with careful reading. First, read the text all the way through. Don't write anything down the first time. Then read the questions – but don't try to answer them yet. Read the text again, keeping the questions in your mind. You will probably spot some of the answers immediately, but don't write them down yet.

- Finally, go through the questions one at a time working out the answers by looking carefully at the text. Write down your answers and check them all carefully. If there are any questions you can't answer or aren't sure about, leave them and carry on. You can go back to the tricky parts later.

3 Improve your skills: Reading

Skimming and scanning are quick ways of finding information in a piece of text.

When you **skim** or **scan**, you don't read every word. Instead, you run your eyes over the text to spot important or relevant words and **phrases**.

Understanding skimming

Skimming means looking through a text very quickly to get an idea of what it is about. You probably skim some texts already. If you look at the TV listings to pick a programme or film to watch, you don't read the descriptions of items that don't interest you – you look for the names of programmes you like.

Without reading all the information, look at the notice quickly to see what dangers there are at this beach.

Skimming skills

1. If the text has a title, this may give you an idea what it is about. The first **sentence** often tells you what a **paragraph** is about, too.

   - What is this text about?

     The title, 'Safety first', tells you it's going to be about safety. The first line tells you the notice is about when it is safe to swim: 'Swimming on this beach is safe at some times of the year.'

2. Run your eyes over the text, looking out for words that tell you what the text is about. Practise highlighting the words that look important.

   - What are the dangers and safety precautions the passage is about? Highlight the key words.

     In early spring, ==dangerous high tides== are signalled by a ==red flag== on the beach. … In late spring and summer, the main ==dangers== are ==sharks and jellyfish==… you should only swim when the ==lifeguard== is on duty. There will be a ==green flag== … Never swim in a ==thunderstorm==. In the autumn the ==sea may be rough==.

3. If you're trying to work out the mood or feeling of a piece of writing, look for words about sounds, smells, sights and feelings.

Safety first

Swimming on this beach is safe at some times of year. In early spring, dangerous high tides are signalled by a red flag on the beach. Don't swim if you see the flag. In late spring and summer, the main dangers are sharks and jellyfish. Don't go in the water in April and July when these creatures most often visit. From May to August you should only swim when the lifeguard is on duty. There will be a green flag on the beach at these times. Never swim in a thunderstorm. In the autumn the sea may be rough. There will be a red flag when it is considered dangerous. If you see someone get into trouble in the water, call the lifeguard on this number: 999. There is a lifebelt under this notice.

Comprehension

Skimming and scanning text

Understanding scanning

Scanning means looking for particular words or information. You look quickly at each sentence or paragraph to see if it's likely to contain the information you need. As you get used to scanning, you'll find the words you're looking for 'jump' out of the text at you.

TRY IT OUT
Dinner time!
Find a menu online for a restaurant you like and skim it to pick the perfect dinner.

- Don't read it carefully – look at the items quickly and read just those that look tasty.

Scanning skills

1 Look for words relating to the sort of information you want to find.
   - Which version of ZombieZoo do you need to have if you want to install Zombie Poodle Attack?

   Look for sentences with 'ZombieZoo' in them – one tells you that you need ZombieZoo2, and you need to upgrade if you have ZombieZoo.

2 Sometimes the information you need may be in a special place. For instance, the ingredients of a food are listed in an information box on the packet.
   - What else does your computer need to run Zombie Poodle Attack?

   You need a DVD drive, 4MB of RAM and 80MB of hard disk space.

   The information about the technical requirements is separate from the text telling you how good the game is.

Zombie Poodle Attack

Zombie Poodle Attack adds new types of zombie dog to ZombieZoo. You can customise the Zombie Poodles in your attack team, choosing their colour, special powers, fur-style and diet. If you have ZombieZoo2, you can add Poodle Attack. If you have ZombieZoo you will need to upgrade to ZombieZoo2 first.

The game needs a DVD drive, 4MB of RAM and 80MB of free hard disk space.

TEST YOURSELF

Skim and scan this article to answer the questions.

Sisters Helen and Angela Macguire surprised police when they caught a criminal red-handed. The girls were playing netball in their driveway when they saw a smartly dressed man fiddling with their neighbour's car. Quick-witted Helen realised he wasn't the owner and threw the netball at him while her little sister called the police. Officers arrived to find the man lying stunned in the driveway. He was taken to hospital and later arrested. A police spokesman said members of the public should not aim to harm criminals, but the girls' quick thinking had saved their neighbour from losing her car.

1 Which of these would be the best title for this newspaper article?
   - A Exciting games in the garden
   - B A deadly header
   - C Car thief foiled by games girls
   - D Football crazy!
   - E Mugger out cold

2 Do the police approve of the public attacking criminals?

21

3 Improve your skills: Reading

Finding information

Most texts are packed with information of different types – the words need to put across this information in the clearest possible way.

Finding information in a text can be easy, or rather tricky. Factual texts often present information clearly, but sometimes they use words that are unfamiliar. Finding information in stories and poems may take a bit of detective work!

Understanding how to search a factual text

Sometimes, the information is easy to see – the text tells you exactly what you need to know. But sometimes you need to think a little and interpret the text. The information you want is not always the main point of the **sentence**.

```
              A house of ice
The ice is compacted – the snow has been pressed together with a
lot of force so that it is solid. The Alaskan Eskimo cuts blocks
from the ice to make the igloo. The serrated knife that he uses
makes it possible to saw through even the hardest blocks of ice.
The Eskimo builder layers his blocks of ice and can cement them
together with water. Although the house is made of ice, it can be
warm inside. It shelters the family from the wind, and the warmth
of their bodies soon heats up the space inside.
```

This description of building an igloo is from the voice-over of a TV programme.

Skills in searching factual texts

1. In descriptive texts or accounts, you might have to read carefully to find the information you need. Look out for words that may lead you to the answer to the test question.
   - What type of knife does the Eskimo builder use?

     *The question is about the knife, so look for this word in the text.
     The third sentence tells you about the Eskimo's knife:*

     'The serrated knife that he uses…'

2. You won't always find the words from the test questions used directly in the extract.
   - Why is the ice very hard?

     The first sentence in the extract explains why the ice is hard: 'compacted' and 'solid' are the clues you need. The ice is made of snow that has been pressed (compacted) and become solid.

3. Sometimes, a sentence that seems to be telling you something else gives you the information you need.
   - Who will live in the house?

     The igloo 'shelters the family from the wind.' This tells you that a family will live in the igloo, but the sentence seems to be about why the igloo is warm – the information about the family is just dropped in while the text explains how the ice house can be warm.

Comprehension

Finding information

4 In an instructional text, the information you need should be given very clearly. There may be a glossary, lists and numbered points to help you; for example, in a recipe the ingredients are clearly listed at the start, and what you need to do is set out in steps.

TRY IT OUT
Adverts
An advert usually tries to make a product seem really good so that you will want it. It can be difficult to find the facts among the words that are encouraging you to buy.

- Choose an advert and underline or highlight the parts that contain factual information.
- Write a list of the things you can tell from this. You might be able to find out the size, colour, price or function of the item, for example.

TEST YOURSELF
Boat crew in trouble
An attempt to copy a historic journey made more than a thousand years ago was abandoned last night. A team of students from Southampton built a boat similar to one Polynesian explorers may once have used. The seven-person crew gave up 200 miles short of their destination and radioed for help.

"We had run out of drinking water", one crew member told our interviewer, "so we had to give up our goal of making it to Hawaii. It's a shame, but we will try again when we can raise the money for another attempt."

1. How many people were in the boat?
    A one **B** two **C** three **D** seven **E** 200
2. Where was the boat supposed to be going?
    A Polynesia **B** Hawaii **C** Southampton
    D France **X** None of the above.
3. When did Polynesian explorers go to Hawaii?

23

3 Improve your skills: Reading

Understanding how to search a fictional text

Stories, poems and plays do not usually present factual information, but they give you information about characters, places, events, moods or feelings. Sometimes you have to work out information from descriptions, or from dialogue (speech).

Chopping wood

Ivan wrapped his scarf tightly around his face against the freezing fog and picked up the axe. He was always scared to chop wood in the dead of winter. Every night, he heard the bears growling with hunger in the forest that surrounded their hut. Every night they seemed to get closer and hungrier. He was sure they were hungry for boys. He was shivering with fright as much as cold when he lifted the latch and stepped outside. Dark gathered around the corners of the hut and between the trees. The wolves would be out soon.

'There is some soup left from yesterday you can have when you come back,' called his grandfather. 'If you add more water, you can stretch it to two bowls and we can share it.' Ivan's tummy rumbled at the thought of soup, even if it was thin. Perhaps he could find some crusts to drop into it, too.

Skills in searching fiction texts

1. It's a good idea to start by working out *who* and *what* a text is about, *where* it is set and *why* the action is taking place. That can help you answer other questions about it.

   - Who is in this story?

     The characters here are a boy called Ivan and his grandfather, and the wolves outside in the forest.

   - What is happening?

     Ivan is getting ready to go outside and chop wood. He is looking forward to soup when he gets back.

   - Why is Ivan shivering?

     He is cold and he is also scared of the wolves that might be outside: he is 'shivering with fright as much as cold'.

2. You can work out some information from what is happening in the story.

   - Where do you think Ivan and his grandfather live?

     Ivan and his grandfather live in a hut in the forest. They live in an area where there are bears and wolves. You may know that Ivan is a Russian name – Russia has a lot of forest, and there are bears and wolves there, so he may live in Russia.

Comprehension

3. Stories often give a lot of extra information while telling you what happens. Look carefully at the description, the **adjectives** and the **adverbs** – these can often help you to work out what is going on, and to 'read between the lines'.

- What is the weather like?

    It is very cold and foggy; the text says that Ivan wraps his scarf 'against the freezing fog'.

4. Your own experience and knowledge are very useful in helping you to read between the lines in a story. You can tell that Ivan is hungry because his tummy rumbles when he thinks about soup.

- Do you think Ivan and his grandfather are rich?

    They are probably poor, as Ivan is looking forward to a supper that sounds quite nasty. He hopes to find a crust, and he has to thin the soup to share it with his grandfather. This suggests they don't have much money for food.

TRY IT OUT

News

Find a short news article in the paper or online.

- What is the article about?
- When and where did the event take place?

TEST YOURSELF

The baby gurgled and waved its podgy arms around. It sat like a fat triangle on the rug, its nappy forming a solid base. Then it squealed loudly and made a lunge for the plastic bricks that Dom was playing with. Dom immediately held them out of the baby's reach. The baby squealed again, but this time it sounded different – it sounded cross. Dom smiled at it, a nasty, leering smile. The baby wasn't fooled and stretched out its hand to try to reach the plastic bricks, but Dom held them high in the air. The baby fidgeted on its bottom, but couldn't move closer. Dom moved further away, trying to tempt the baby into toppling over. At that moment, Rita came in, and Dom quickly hid the bricks behind his back.

'Are you two having a nice time?' she asked.

'Lovely,' Dom lied. As soon as Rita turned her back, Dom poked his tongue out at the baby. The baby waved its arms again, still wanting the bricks, and began to cry. Dom smiled, and held the bricks even more tightly, but just where the baby could see them.

1. What is the baby wearing?

    A a sleepsuit **B** a dress **C** a nappy **D** nothing **E** a t-shirt

2. Which statement about whether Dom likes the baby is true?

    A Yes – he smiles at the baby.

    B No – he pushes the baby over.

    C Yes – he says he is having a lovely time.

    D No – he holds toys where the baby can't get them.

    X None of the above.

3. Do you think Dom is a nice person?

Deduction and inference

3 Improve your skills: Reading

Both deduction and inference questions ask you to look for clues in the text to come to a conclusion.

Deduction is reaching a conclusion based on clear information you are given. **Inference** is more subtle; it involves using clues from the text *and* your previous knowledge to decide what is most *likely* to be true.

Understanding deduction

You use deduction all the time without even realising it when you interpret texts you read. It involves putting together and interpreting evidence from the text.

If you are planning to visit the cinema, you may read the film descriptions in the paper.

TOY STORY 3 3D

What dangers await Buzz and Woody now Andy is going to college?

The garbage truck crunches its way violently through unwanted toys as all the other kids clean out their rooms. Dark forces are at work in Sunnyside nursery where no toy has ever been known to leave…

Deduction skills

1. A deduction question will give you all the information you need to draw the right conclusion. Look for clues in the text.
   - How old is Andy?

     Andy is going to college, so he must be over 16.

2. Words that affect your feelings or emotions help you work out what emotional impact the text is aiming at.
   - Will the film be romantic or scary?

     'Dangers', 'violently' and 'dark forces' tell us that there may be some scary moments in the film. No words suggest that the film will be romantic.

3. You can use deduction to work out how things are likely to turn out.
   - What does the author want us to think about Sunnyside nursery?

     As 'dark forces are at work in Sunnyside nursery' we can deduce that something bad is likely to happen there.

TRY IT OUT

Adverts

Adverts encourage us to make deductions and inferences about how good a product is.

- Pick out the descriptive words in an advert.
- Now change the descriptive words so that the advert has the opposite meaning.

Comprehension

Understanding inference

Inference is responding to suggestions in a text to come to a conclusion. Instead of finding definite statements, you have to draw conclusions that seem likely, based on evidence in the text.

In the park

Benji didn't want to sit next to the old man, but there were no other spaces. The man had dirty clothes and matted hair. He had spilled food down his front and there was mud all over his shoes. The shoes had holes in and they weren't a pair. One was brown and one was black.

At that moment, a film crew came round the corner and a director shouted 'Action!' The man started to speak to a camera.

Inference skills

1. Inference involves deciding what is likely from the text you have in front of you.
   - Reading the first **paragraph**, what type of person do you think the old man is? Why?

   It sounds as if the old man is a tramp. We work this out from the description, and because Benji doesn't want to sit near him.

2. Sometimes a writer encourages us to infer something that may not be true. Adverts want us to infer that a product is really good, for example.
   - Did you make the wrong inference when you read the first paragraph? What do you think about the old man after reading the second paragraph?

   The second paragraph suggests that he is an actor. But we could still be wrong – the text doesn't give hard evidence. The man might be a tramp who is being interviewed by a TV crew.

TEST YOURSELF

Red Riding Hood swung her leather-clad leg over her Harley Davidson and revved up the engine, drowning out her mother's voice.

RRH roared off into the forest, then screeched to a halt in front of a very startled grey wolf crossing the road.

"Get out of the way, fleabag! I'm in a hurry to see my gran, who's allegedly dying and might leave me a packet," screamed RRH.

The wolf's eyes brightened as he thought of the delicious granny snack. Then he rushed ahead of RRH to gobble up the granny and wait in bed for a younger and more succulent dessert. The Harley's wheels spun and gravel sprayed everywhere as RRH made a dramatic stop outside her Gran's cottage. The milk on the doorstep made RRH suspicious; the drawn curtains clinched it. Something was up!

1. How do you know that the wolf is planning to eat RRH?
2. What do you think Red Riding Hood is likely to be wearing?

   A A red dress **B** Cycling shorts **C** Leather trousers

   D Fur jacket **E** Leggings

Deduction and inference

3 Improve your skills: Reading

Organisation of text

The organisation of a text is the way it is arranged in sentences and paragraphs, and how the parts of the text are linked together.

How a piece of writing is organised can help you understand its meaning and purpose. Most texts follow a clear sequence, but some – like poems – have a more complicated or surprising organisation.

Understanding how text is organised

When you write a story, you have to make sure it has a beginning, a middle and an end. A text usually has a natural order, whether it follows a story, tells events in order or gives instructions in the sequence you need to follow them. The writer organises a text by choosing the order of the **sentences** and using suitable words to link them together.

Granny's war pig

When I was very small, our country was at war and there wasn't much food. My mother kept a pig, which we fed with a few scraps – not many, as we weren't allowed to leave our food. Everyone in the street helped to feed our pig. When the pig grew good and fat, we all walked in procession to Mr Taylor's, leading the pig on a piece of rope. The pig didn't have a clue what was going to happen, of course, and enjoyed the walk, snuffling the gutters and hedges. But I did. After the butcher did the terrible deed, he carved it up and everyone had a share. We had the biggest share because it was our pig. I cried all the way home. But I still ate the bacon.

Skills in organising texts

1 The title and any subheadings help you see what the text is going to be about and how it's organised.
2 The opening gives you an idea of what the text will be about. It may set the scene, or explain what the text will cover.

- When do the events of this **recount** text take place?

    The opening tells us it's about events that happened a long time ago, during a war:

    'When I was very small, our country was at war…'

Comprehension

Organisation of text

3. Words used to connect sentences and **phrases** organise the text into a sequence.
   - Look for time **connectives** that tell you the order of events, such as 'before', 'after', 'when', 'then'.

   'When the pig grew good and fat…'

   'After the butcher did the terrible deed…'

4. Sometimes, the text organisation works to incorporate flashbacks, build suspense or create atmosphere.
   - Do we know who Mr Taylor is at this point in the extract?

   '…we all walked in procession to Mr Taylor's…'

   We don't know who Mr Taylor is, and the description of the journey doesn't give any clues. This keeps us reading to see what will happen.

   - Look at which sentences are put next to each other. Are there links between them? Words such as 'then', 'and', 'so' and 'but' can create connections or surprise.

   'We had the biggest share because it was our pig. I cried all the way home. But I still ate the bacon.'

5. Changes in **font** style such as **bold** or *italics*, are often used to make text stand out or emphasise a point.

TRY IT OUT
Instructions

Lots of things have sets of instructions. Find a toy with instructions, or a recipe book. There might be pictures to show you what to do as well as words. The pictures are part of the text, too.

- Change the order of the instructions. Is the text still useful?
- Be careful about cutting up instructions without permission. Your mum might not be happy if you cut up her favourite book!

TEST YOURSELF

It's raining birds!

Residents of a small town in Arkansas were astonished to find dead birds falling from the sky. Over one evening and night, 3000 dead birds rained down on the town – and experts have no idea why.

On New Year's Day, local people woke to find dead blackbirds scattered all over the town. Experts called in to examine them were baffled. Suggestions as to what killed the birds included pesticides, fireworks, thunderstorms, hail, and flying into buildings. But none of these could explain the large number of deaths.

'It remains a mystery,' said a spokesman. 'We don't know what killed the birds, or why they are concentrated in such a small area.'

Bizarrely, reports of mass deaths of fish, birds, crabs and other animals have flooded in from around the world since New Year. Scientists have not been able to come up with an explanation.

1. How does the text organisation make the article interesting and draw you in to reading it?

2. What does the article encourage you to think about the 'rain of birds'?
   - **A** that the birds were killed by pesticides
   - **B** that the birds flew into buildings
   - **C** that scientists can work out how the birds died
   - **D** that the 'rain of birds' is a mystery
   - **E** that this is a very common occurrence and should not be thought unusual

Different styles of fiction writing are listed on pages 76–77.
Pages 68–75 explain the common structures used in non-fiction writing.

3 Improve your skills: Reading

The effect of a text is created by the words the writer uses – the use of language.

Looking closely at the language a writer chooses helps you to see how a text creates an effect or serves its purpose.

Understanding how a writer uses language

The writer's choice of words and the way he or she puts them together help to produce feeling, atmosphere, humour, tone, style and other effects in a text. A writer will often choose more precise **nouns** and **verbs** to avoid using an **adjective** or **adverb** – so 'whispered' instead of 'said quietly'. The associations of a word can bring extra meaning to a text: something that is 'blood red' has a different feel from something 'strawberry coloured'. Whether the text has short or long **sentences** also adds to its effect.

Wreckers

Jamilla raced across the field, her hair flying in her face and blinding her so that she often stumbled. She had to get away, she couldn't bear to stay and watch. It would be awful, horrible, heartbreaking. She had played in the old woman's house so many times, so happily, and she felt all her memories would be reduced to rubble along with the building. There was no need to knock it down to make space for new houses – why couldn't the house just be sold to a family? The dead woman's son was mean and greedy and the only reason he could possibly want to sell his childhood home to developers was to make money. Already the rumble of the wrecker's lorry followed her across the field.

Skills in how writers use language

1. The title of a piece of writing sets up expectations of what it will be about or what it will be like. The title 'Wreckers' tells us the story is likely to be about destruction in some form. You don't expect a cheery or funny story from this title.

2. Look at the important words in the text – the **nouns**, **adjectives**, **verbs** and **adverbs**.
   - What is the effect of the sentence 'It would be awful, horrible, heartbreaking'?

     By using lots of adjectives, the writer stresses how horrible it will be for Jamilla. It also makes it seem as though Jamilla is searching for the right word to express just how terrible it seems to her.

3. Try to work out who is 'speaking' from the language used. By choosing words a character might say, the writer suggests this is what the character is thinking.
   - Can you find a bit that looks as if it is supposed to be Jamilla's words?

     'There was no need to knock it down to make space for new houses – why couldn't the house just be sold to a family? The dead woman's son was mean and greedy and the only reason he could possibly want to sell his childhood home to developers was to make money'. These are Jamilla's thoughts, though the writer does not say 'Jamilla thought…'

Comprehension

How writers use language

4. The language in a persuasive text will try to get you to agree with the writer. It might, for instance, suggest you already agree, flatter you, or suggest you are foolish if you disagree. It might use questions, expecting you to agree with the voice in the story. If the writer doesn't give or expect an answer to the question, it's called a **rhetorical question**.

- Can you find a rhetorical question in the passage?

    'Why couldn't the house just be sold to a family?' is a rhetorical question. Jamilla thinks it could be sold to a family, and wants us to think so too.

TRY IT OUT

Changing poems

Choose a funny poem that you like.

- Underline or highlight the nouns, adjectives, verbs and adverbs in the poem.
- Change them all to other words that have similar meanings. How does it make the poem different?

Try the example opposite.

I like peanut butter
I like jam and bread
I like eating chocolate when I'm standing on my head
I hate painful pimples
I hate itchy spots
I hate it when my sister cries and ties her hair in knots

Vote for Adrian!

Adrian would make the perfect environment representative for Year 6.

He lives on a farm, so he knows lots about the environment. He cycles or walks to school – no petrol fumes there! As well as being popular and well known in the school, Adrian is intelligent and confident, features which will help him persuade teachers and parents to toe the line, leave their cars at home and cut waste in lunch boxes.

As your environment rep, Adrian will work to make your school a nicer place to be AND friendly to the planet. Vote for Adrian – you know it makes sense!

TEST YOURSELF

1. What is the effect of the phrase 'As your environment rep'?
2. What effect does the writer create with the phrase 'you know it makes sense'?
    - **A** It makes us think Adrian is sensible.
    - **B** It makes us think Adrian believes we are sensible.
    - **C** We believe Adrian will adopt sensible policies.
    - **D** It suggests we already know it is sensible to vote for Adrian.
    - **E** It suggests we know that going to school by car is sensible.

Writer's viewpoint

3 Improve your skills: Reading

Many texts are written from a particular point of view.

Working out the writer's point of view helps you to decide how reliable a non-fiction text is and what it is aiming to do. Sometimes the writer states their point of view clearly, but sometimes you have to work it out from the language they use and try to separate the facts from their **opinion**.

Understanding a writer's point of view

If a text is **objective** it does not present a particular point of view but tries to be impartial – to present different views equally. A **subjective** piece of writing is coloured by the writer's view. The writer may be open about their view, or may use language subtly to persuade you to agree with them. Understanding the writer's point of view helps you to separate facts from opinions in a text.

The climate time-bomb

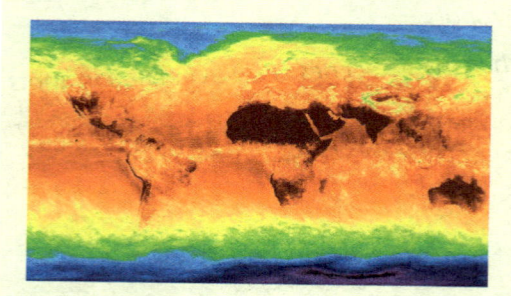

You would have to have been living in a cave – or worse – to have missed the media fuss over recent years about the environment. Senior scientists agree that humans are damaging the world beyond repair, and we're doing nothing to stop it. We use too much fuel and other resources, we're careless with our waste and spoil the environment with our greed. Global temperatures may rise by 5°C in the next hundred years. The result will be rising sea levels and drier land in many places. Human and animal populations will be devastated, lives ruined, habitats destroyed. Low-lying land will be flooded and lost to the sea, leaving millions homeless. Deserts will spread, and ferocious wars will start as people struggle for survival, fighting for water and usable land. We need to take action now – and that means making changes to our lives as well as pressing our governments to take action.

Skills in identifying a writer's point of view

1 The writer might say 'I think' or 'In my opinion' or might present their view through what they say.
   - Does the writer openly state their point of view?
     The writer doesn't say that they are stating an opinion or belief – they present all that they say as facts.
   - Can you judge the general view put forward in the text?
     The writer believes that people have caused climate change and it will have serious results.

2 The text might use experts or statistics as evidence to support the view it presents.
   - What evidence does the passage use to persuade us that the writer's view is correct?
     The writer refers to 'senior scientists' – we are likely to take their view seriously, so this adds weight to the writer's point of view.

Comprehension

Writer's viewpoint

3 Look for words that show strong emotion or emphasise a point. The text might use positive or negative words instead of neutral words.
   - Find some words that produce a strong emotional effect in the passage.
     There are lots of these. Examples are 'careless', 'greed', 'devastated', 'ruined', 'destroyed', 'ferocious', and 'struggle'.

4 Look for the writer trying to win you over by using 'we' to suggest you already agree with them, or by suggesting a different view is foolish.
   - Find some examples of the writer trying to win you over in this passage
     'We use too much fuel' and 'we're careless with our waste'.

5 It can sometimes be hard to tell whether something is objective fact – something everyone agrees on – or whether it is an opinion. Make sure you can tell the difference between fact and opinion.
   - Can you find one fact and one opinion in the text?
     'Global temperatures may rise by 5°C in the next hundred years' – this is a fact.
     'We need to take action now' – this is an opinion.
   - In a story or poem, the point of view of the narrator, or the 'I' character, does not always match the views or opinions of the writer. There is more than one way of looking at any event.

TRY IT OUT

Miss Muffet

Little Miss Muffet, sat on a tuffet

Eating her curds and whey.

Along came a spider

And sat down beside her

And frightened Miss Muffet away.

- Write this story from Miss Muffet's point of view.
- Rewrite it from the spider's point of view.

TEST YOURSELF

School uniform is often promoted as a great leveller. If children all have to wear the same clothes, the argument goes, they will not be able to compete with each other to have the most costly or stylish outfits. But is this true? No. Children easily make tiny differences in the style of a school uniform. Baggier or tighter trousers, a tight or loose jumper, a pleated or straight skirt – there are countless ways of varying a uniform. Why not leave children free to express themselves? Clothes are a way of making a statement about who you are. Children in uniform are stifled and their individuality is suffocated. Children can't flourish and grow comfortable with themselves if their character is crushed, if they are made to seem the same as all other children.

1 Does the writer think children should wear school uniforms?

2 What is the writer's view of school uniform?

   A It is a good idea as it is a great leveller.

   B It is a bad idea because it stops children expressing their characters.

   C It is a good idea because children then won't compete to wear expensive clothes.

   D It is a good idea because children can choose to wear baggy or tight trousers.

   E It is a bad idea because school uniforms are expensive.

3 Improve your skills: Reading

Traditional and social context

Texts reflect the societies and cultures in which they are written.

Knowing about the time and place a text was written helps you to understand it.

Understanding context

Context is the time and place in which a text was written. Every society has beliefs and general knowledge that most people take for granted. These give the social context. For example, in 1850 people usually travelled in vehicles pulled by horses, so they appear a lot in stories. If a story mentioned someone going in a horse-drawn vehicle in 2010 the writer would be making a special point.

Sometimes a text has a traditional form of opening. Many fairy tales start 'Once upon a time…' Fables tell a short story and then explain the moral it is showing. Look out for traditional contexts like this – they tell you what type of story it is.

Review the different styles of fiction writing on pages 76–77 and the common structures used in non-fiction writing on pages 68–75.

Skills in identifying the context

1. Look for clues that tell you the time and place in which the text was written. The title of the text may sometimes help. The things and people in the text and the way people talk to each other can give you clues about the social and historical context.

   - What in this text tells you it is not about modern Britain?

   The man goes in a boat rowed by prisoners to a prison ship. This doesn't happen today in Britain. The men use flaming torches – today we use electric lights.

2. Look at the attitudes and viewpoint shown in the text. This may reflect the time and place it was written.

   - What is the attitude towards the prisoners? Is this a modern British attitude?

   The prisoners are treated badly – they have to row the boat, they live in a prison ship and they wear iron chains: 'the prison-ship seemed in my young eyes to be ironed like the prisoners'. Someone growls at them as though they were dogs. Modern attitudes and behaviour towards prisoners in Britain are not as harsh.

A prison ship

The boat had returned, and his guard were ready, so we followed him to the landing-place made of rough stakes and stones, and saw him put into the boat, which was rowed by a crew of convicts like himself. No one seemed surprised to see him, or interested in seeing him, or glad to see him, or sorry to see him, or spoke a word, except that somebody in the boat growled as if to dogs, "Give way, you!" which was the signal for the dip of the oars. By the light of the torches, we saw the black Hulk lying out a little way from the mud of the shore, like a wicked Noah's ark. Cribbed and barred and moored by massive rusty chains, the prison-ship seemed in my young eyes to be ironed like the prisoners. We saw the boat go alongside, and we saw him taken up the side and disappear. Then, the ends of the torches were flung hissing into the water, and went out, as if it were all over with him.

Great Expectations, by Charles Dickens

Comprehension

Traditional and social context

3 A writer might make assumptions about what the reader knows. These assumptions are based in the social and historical context of the writing.

- What assumption does the writer make when choosing the phrase 'a wicked Noah's ark'?

The writer assumed his readers would know the Bible story of Noah's ark, so he was writing in a time and place when most people were Christians.

TRY IT OUT
Cartoons
Many cartoons depend on readers knowing about the same things as the cartoonist. They might make fun of a famous person, comment on a recent event or develop a story using the same characters every week.

- Look at a cartoon and work out what you need to know for it to make sense.
- Would someone 200 years in the past or future understand the cartoon?

TEST YOURSELF

Once upon a time there was a beautiful girl who lived with her old father in a village in the forest. They were poor, but happy.

One day, the father had to go to the nearby town on business. He asked his daughter if there was anything she wanted as a present. Knowing they were poor, the girl asked for only a single rose, which she thought he would be able to pick from a rose tree.

On his way back, the father saw blood-red roses on a rose bush that leaned over a high wall. Thinking to take just one for his daughter, he followed the wall to a locked iron gate. Behind the gate was a huge, dark tower.

1 How do you know this is going to be a fairy tale?
2 List some things in the passage that you have seen in other fairy tales.
3 Do you think a good or bad person lives in the castle?
4 Will the story have a happy ending?

FANTASTIC FACTS
Where and when
The time and place in which a story is set is not always the same as the context in which it was written. A modern writer could set a book in Ancient Rome, but the social and historical context in which it was written would still be modern Britain. This means, for example, that the writer has not been to gladiatorial games and probably doesn't really approve of feeding people to lions, whatever the text may say!

3 Improve your skills: Reading

Introducing grammar

Grammar is the set of rules that govern how words work together to make writing easy to follow. A grammar test gives you the chance to identify and use different types of words.

Grammar questions test that you can use grammar correctly so that your writing is clear. They also test your understanding of how grammar is used in a variety of ways to create interesting effects.

What to expect

In the test, there will be questions about how grammar works, and you will also need to use grammar correctly in your own writing. In some papers, all the questions will be multiple-choice and you will need to choose the correct option to make sense of the **sentence**.

Grammar questions might ask you to find examples of different types of words – such as **nouns** or **verbs** – or to spot grammatical mistakes in a piece of writing and correct them. You will also need to know how to structure sentences; what the different parts of speech are; how to use parts of speech and how writers use language to make their writing more effective and enjoyable. You might need to answer questions such as these:

1 Which of these words is an **adjective**?

    A banana **B** suddenly **C** perhaps **D** smelly **E** swimming

'Smelly' (answer **D**) is an adjective. You can use it in front of a noun to say something more about the noun, as in 'smelly toilets'.

2 Which of these sentences does *not* include an **adverb**?

    A The horse trotted briskly to the stable.

    B The knight polished his armour with a cloth and oil.

    C Rabbits often dig burrows in my garden.

    D The whale dived right to the bottom of the sea.

    E Paula put the hot cup down quickly.

Sentence **B** does not contain an adverb; there is nothing to tell you how the knight polished his armour, only what he used to do it. The other adverbs are 'briskly', 'often', 'right' and 'quickly'.

Grammar skills

1 Grammatical writing is in complete sentences, so you need to be clear about what a sentence is.

    Sentences are complete units – each sentence must make sense on its own.

2 A sentence must always have a verb and a **subject**.

    A verb is a word that tells you about an action.

    The subject is a thing or person that does something.

- The monster slept.

Grammar

Introducing grammar

3 Some sentences also have an **object**.
- Shahrukh ate a pear.

The object in this example is the pear. It is the thing or person that something happens to – in this case, it gets eaten. It may be a place, a thing, a feeling or a person.

A sentence must have a subject and a verb, but it doesn't need to have an object.

4 Read the extract, then read through the following questions and explanations.

A chimney sweep

Once upon a time there was a little chimney sweep, and his name was Tom. That is a short name, and you have heard it before, so you will not have much trouble in remembering it. He lived in a great town in the North country, where there were plenty of chimneys to sweep, and plenty of money for Tom to earn and his master to spend. He could not read nor write, and did not care to do either; and he never washed himself, for there is no water up the court where he lived. He had never been taught to say his prayers.

Adapted from **The Water-babies**, by Charles Kingsley

In the test, you will be expected to answer questions like these:

- Which of these words is a noun?

    A short   B heard   C chimney

    D never   E where

    A noun is the name of a thing, person or abstract concept. 'Chimney' (answer C) is a noun.

- Which of these could have been used as a complete, properly written sentence?

    A Tom was a chimney sweep he lived in the town

    B he didn't always have enough food

    C did Tom have enough money?

    D There was no running water where.

    E There were lots of chimneys to sweep.

    A *sentence must start with a* **capital letter***, end with a full stop, a* **question mark** *or an* **exclamation mark** *and must make sense on its own.*
    Only answer E does all these: There were lots of chimneys to sweep.

What you will learn

In this section you will learn about these grammar topics…
- parts of speech
- figurative language
- how to start a sentence in different ways
- how to make sure the verb and subject agree
- how to use verb tenses consistently.

TIPS FOR SUCCESS

Getting grammar

When you write your own texts or answer a grammar question, you will need to know:
- what is needed to make a sentence and how to start and end sentences
- what the different parts of speech are
- how to use verbs properly so that your writing is consistent.

3 Improve your skills: Reading

'Parts of speech' are the different types of words you may find in a sentence.

Different **parts of speech** do different work in a piece of writing.

Understanding parts of speech

The names for things or people are **nouns** – for example, 'crow', 'holiday', 'bucket'. Words that tell you more about a noun are **adjectives**. Examples are 'brown', 'thin' or 'angry'.

Words that tell you what someone or something is doing are **verbs**, for example 'run', 'eat', 'know'. Words that tell you more about how the action is done are **adverbs**, for example 'greedily', 'quickly', 'often'.

Sometimes a noun can be used as an adjective. 'Birthday' is a noun in the **sentence** 'Today is my birthday', but it's used as an adjective in the phrase 'This is my birthday cake'.

Sock puppets

You can easily make a puppet from a sock – it's a good way to have fun with an old sock! You will need…

- a sock
- felt
- wool
- scissors
- glue, or a needle and thread
- a pen.

Put the sock over your hand and mark with the pen where you want the eyes to be.

Make fabric eyes or use some 'googly eyes' from a shop and stick or stitch them on.

Next, use the wool to make funny hair for your puppet.

Carefully trim the wool with the scissors – don't cut yourself.

Here's a puppet we made; ours is called Poppy.

Skills in identifying parts of speech

1. There are different types of noun. A noun that is the name of a real thing is called a **common noun**. The names of people or places have a **capital letter** and are called **proper nouns**. The names of concepts or ideas, such as 'love' or 'anger', are **abstract nouns**.
   - Can you find two common nouns, a proper noun and an abstract noun in the passage?

     There are a lot of common nouns, including 'puppet', 'felt', 'scissors', 'sock' and 'eyes'. There is only one proper noun – 'Poppy' – and one abstract noun – 'fun'.

2. An adjective tells you a bit more about the noun, such as 'a brown cow'. It usually comes just before the noun it describes, but they can be separated: 'the cow in the field is brown'.
   - See if you can spot these noun/adjective pairs. The adjectives are underlined below.

     Old sock; googly eyes; funny hair.

Grammar

Parts of speech

3. **Verbs** tell you what is happening, such as 'make', 'cut', and 'stick'. The words 'am', 'is', 'are', 'was', 'were' and 'would' are parts of the verb 'to be'. 'To be' and 'to have' can also be used with other verbs, such as 'I am going out'.

4. **Adverbs** tell you more about a verb. They can tell you how, when or where the action is done – 'run quickly', 'come early', 'exercise often' and 'play indoors'. Adverbs often end in '-ly', such as 'slowly' or 'happily'.

   - Look for this adverb/verb pair in the text. The adverb is underlined below.
     <u>Easily</u> make.

5. **Pronouns** relate to people or things. The **personal pronouns** such as 'I' and 'they' tell you who or what is being talked about. **Possessive pronouns** tell you who or what something belongs to, like 'my' and 'her'.

   - Look for the personal and possessive pronouns that are used in the passage.
     Personal pronouns used are 'you' and 'we'; possessive pronouns used are 'your' and 'ours'.

6. Words that link nouns, pronouns and **phrases** to other parts of a sentence are **prepositions**. They include 'in', 'before', 'during' 'without' and 'on'.

   - Look for these prepositions in the text: 'have fun with'; 'googly eyes' from a shop'; 'funny hair for your puppet'. The prepositions are underlined below.
     'have fun <u>with</u>'; 'googly eyes' <u>from</u> a shop'; 'funny hair <u>for</u> your puppet'.

7. Words and phrases that join all the other parts of the sentence are called **connectives** or **conjunctions**. Examples are 'and', 'but', 'however', and 'on the other hand'.

   Comparatives and **superlatives** compare a characteristic of one thing to that of another. Comparatives include bigger, higher, quieter; superlatives include biggest, highest, quietest.

   The connectives in the passage are 'and', 'or' and 'next'.

   *The little words 'a', 'an' and 'the' which go with a noun are called '**articles**'. They tell you whether the writer means a specific thing (the) or any instance of a thing (a/an). 'The' is the **definite article** and 'a'/'an' is the **indefinite article**.*

TRY IT OUT

Story

You can find parts of speech in any piece of writing.

- Pick a story you like. Change the nouns and adjectives in the first three lines to others. Change the verbs and adverbs – then the story will say something completely different!

TEST YOURSELF

Alice was beginning to get very tired of sitting by her sister on the bank and of having nothing to do: once or twice she had peeped into the book her sister was reading, but it had no pictures or conversations in it, "and what is the use of a book," thought Alice, "without pictures or conversations?"

Alice in Wonderland, by Lewis Carroll

1. Underline or highlight all the nouns in yellow; underline or highlight all the adjectives in blue; underline or highlight all the verbs in pink. Circle all the pronouns.

2. Which one of these is an adverb?

   A use   **B** without   **C** nothing

   D twice   **E** peeped

39

Figurative language

3 Improve your skills: Reading

Lots of texts use figurative language such as imagery or sound patterns to create special effects.

Figurative language is a good way of making the reader see connections between things, or see things in a new way.
It can make sights, sounds and feelings more vivid and exciting.

Understanding figurative language

Writers use many ways to get across what they mean and to create an effect for the reader. They use not just the literal meanings of words, but their sounds and associations, and use words to create an image in the reader's mind.

If the text pretends one thing is another, it's using a **metaphor**: 'her anger was a hard knot in her stomach'. Anger isn't really a knot in the stomach, but it can feel like it and imagining a knot makes the anger seem real when you read about it. A **simile** compares two things but doesn't pretend they are the same: as 'green *as* grass', or 'roaring *like* a lion'.

Other types of figurative language use sound to make a striking effect or make readers think differently about something.

Skills in figurative language

1. You can spot similes because they often use 'as' or 'like'.
   - Can you find a simile in the poem?
     The poet compares himself to a cloud ('I wander'd lonely as a cloud') and says there are as many daffodils as stars in the Milky Way.

2. The poet describes the daffodils as dancing, but they are not really dancing.
   - Is this a metaphor or a simile?
     It's a metaphor – it would be a simile if he said they moved <u>like</u> dancers.

3. **Personification** is a type of metaphor. It gives human actions, thoughts or feelings to things that are not human: 'the sun struggled to come out from behind the clouds'. The sun can't really struggle – only people or animals can struggle.
   - What is personified in the poem? How?
     The daffodils are personified as a 'crowd' or 'host' and as dancers. The poet takes it even further in the line 'Tossing their heads in sprightly dance'.

Daffodils

I wander'd lonely as a cloud
That floats on high o'er vales and hills,
When all at once I saw a crowd,
A host, of golden daffodils;
Beside the lake, beneath the trees,
Fluttering and dancing in the breeze.

Continuous as the stars that shine
And twinkle on the Milky Way,
They stretch'd in never-ending line
Along the margin of a bay:
Ten thousand saw I at a glance,
Tossing their heads in sprightly dance.

Daffodils, by William Wordsworth

Grammar

Figurative language

4. Sound patterns are a type of figurative language, too. If several words start with same letter, the sound pattern is called **alliteration**. For example, '**sl**ugs **sl**ithered though the **sl**op'. If a word sounds like what it describes, that is **onomatopoeia** – 'whisper', 'crack' and 'flicker' are examples. **Assonance** uses the same **vowel** sound close together: 'str**e**tch'd in n**e**ver-ending line'. **Rhyme** is a type of sound pattern you are probably very used to.

- Can you find some sound patterns in the poem and identify them?

   There is rhyme in the poem: cloud/crowd; hills/daffodils; trees/breeze; shine/line; Way/bay; glance/dance.

   There is assonance: floats/o'er; beneath/trees/breeze; twinkle/Milky; thousand/at/a/glance.

   You might have thought of 'fluttering' as an example of onomatopoeia.

TRY IT OUT

Write your own

- Copy these sentences and fill in the spaces to make similes:

   The spot on his nose was as … as a …

   The banana had been in his drawer for four weeks. It smelled like …

- Complete this sentences to make personification:

   His disgraceful clothes called out for …

- Complete this sentence using alliteration:

   The … porcupine … in the …

TEST YOURSELF

Jake opened his eyes to a square of blue sky. A flag flapped lazily at the mast, the skull and crossbones leering down at him. He closed his eyes again, confused. His head hurt – it felt as if someone were hammering nails into his brain – bang, bang, bang – and he couldn't think. Out of the corner of his eye, he caught sight of a snake of rope slithering across the deck to his left and there, tied to the end of it, was a human foot, followed by a leg, and then the bulk of Captain Williams. He had his arms folded and his eyes closed, as peaceful as a sleeping cat. Drunk, thought Jake. Too much rum. Again.

1. Find a metaphor in the text. What does it make you imagine or think?
2. Which of these is an example of alliteration?

   A as peaceful as a sleeping cat

   B slithering

   C a flag flapped lazily

   D the skull and crossbones leering down

   X None of them.

3 Improve your skills: Reading

Starting sentences

To make your writing interesting and fresh, start your sentences in different ways.

When most of the **sentences** start the same way, it may be dull and difficult to read even if what it says is interesting.

Understanding how to start sentences

To keep people reading, vary the way you start your sentences. You can begin with a **noun**, an **adjective**, a **verb**, an **adverb** or a **preposition**. It's good to start a story in the middle of something exciting, or with someone speaking. Choose a way to start that suits the feeling you want to get across.

Wolf alert!

Once upon a time there were three little pigs who lived in a forest. One pig was very sensible. He wore sensible shoes, cleaned his teeth every morning and every night, went to bed early and lived in a house of bricks. Another little pig was a bit scatty. Sometimes he remembered to clean his teeth, but he wore odd socks and he rarely went to bed before midnight. The last little pig was far from sensible. He never had any clean clothes, hadn't cleaned his teeth since Tuesday and didn't know what time he went to bed, as his clock was broken. Friday was a peaceful day, until…
Hurtling through the forest far too fast, a big, bad wolf crashed into the café where the pigs were having breakfast. Chairs and tables flew in all directions. Wolf fur and breakfast mixed together.

'Run!' cried the sensible pig, and made for the door. The scatty pig looked for his bag; the silly pig carried on eating his toasted bun.

Skills in starting sentences

1 The start of the first sentence in a text is particularly important. Many traditional stories start with 'Once upon a time'.
   - Which part of speech is this sentence starting with?
   - How does this start make you feel about the story?

   It starts with a preposition. Another example would be 'On Wednesday…'

   It's a familiar and reassuring start. A sentence that begins by telling you the time or **setting** does not feel urgent or exciting. You know this is going to be like a fairy tale because you recognise the starting **phrase**.

Grammar

Starting sentences

2. Starting a sentence with an action word (or verb) is a good way of making it lively.
   - Which is the liveliest sentence? How does it start?

   'Hurtling through the forest…' is the most exciting sentence. It starts with a verb.

3. A sentence that starts with a noun or an adjective tells you immediately what or who the sentence will be about. Sentences often start with a name. In your own stories, try not to start too many sentences with the character's name, as it will get a bit dull.
   - Find a sentence that starts with an adjective and one that starts with a noun. Which sentence draws you in more quickly?

   'One pig…' starts with an adjective; the sentence 'Chairs and tables…' starts with a noun. It gets down to work immediately, so it draws us in easily.

4. Starting a sentence with speech makes it exciting and draws the reader in. It is also refreshing, as it changes the 'voice'.
   - Can you find a sentence that starts with speech?

   'Run!' cried the sensible pig

5. It helps to keep readers interested if you make your sentences different lengths, too.

TRY IT OUT
Changing stories

The way a story starts sets up your expectations.

- Find a story. How does the first sentence start – with a noun, adjective, verb, adverb or preposition?
- Rewrite the sentence using a different type of word to start it. Make sure the sentence means the same.

TEST YOURSELF

Leeches dropped from the trees onto my head and poisonous snakes slithered away from my feet. Everywhere I put my hand, an insect or scorpion scurried away. If you're a bit nervous, Borneo is probably not the best holiday destination for you. Trekking through forest packed with animals set on killing me is not really my idea of fun, and I can see why you might like to avoid it. Hairy spiders are the least of your worries here. Things are not always what they seem, though. I ran away from things that looked deadly, but often they turned out to be harmless. And sometimes I was rather relaxed over things that really were dangerous, so you should take a good guide with you.

But however fierce or fearsome the beasts of the jungle, Borneo is beautiful. 'Welcome to Borneo,' my taxi driver said at the airport – and I have felt welcome. I wouldn't have missed it for the world.

1. Which sentence starts with a verb?
   - A Leeches dropped from the trees…
   - B If you're a bit nervous…
   - C Trekking through forest…
   - D I ran away…
   - X None of them.

2. Which type of word starts the first sentence? What is the effect of starting the article with this sentence?

43

Agreement in sentences

3 Improve your skills: Reading

Agreement means that the different parts of a sentence go together properly.

Verbs must agree in number and in **tense**. This means that your **subject** (the **noun** or **pronoun**) and verb must both be **singular** or both **plural**, and that the tense of the verbs must be consistent.

Understanding agreement of number

In a simple **sentence**, it's quite easy to make sure the subject and verb agree, but it can get complicated in longer sentences. Sometimes there are other words in between and it can be a bit harder to keep track. The general rule is that a singular subject (you are talking about one thing) needs a singular verb, and a plural subject (you are talking about more than one thing) needs a plural verb.

Skills in agreement of number

1. A subject that is single takes a singular verb, and a plural subject takes a plural verb.
   - Find simple examples of a singular and plural subject/verb pairs in the poem.

   'A fish breaks' is an example of a singular noun and verb; 'branches wave' is an example of a plural noun and verb.

2. Even if there are a lot of words in between the subject and the verb, they must still agree.

   'Everything else on the river and the riverbank is'. The words in between don't change the verb.

3. Some words can be a bit harder to work out.
   - Find the verbs that go with 'people', 'everything' and 'nothing'. Are they singular or plural?

   'People lie' – this is plural, as there are several or many people.

   'Everything is still' – this is singular; it means 'every single thing'.

   'Nothing moves' – nothing goes with a singular verb, and so does 'none'. 'None' really means 'not one' – if you wrote 'not one' it would be obvious that you need a singular verb.

4. If there is more than one subject, joined with 'and', the subject counts as plural.
   - Find a line with a subject that is more than one thing.

   'Bird and butterfly' – these are the subject of the plural verb 'are'.

Willows

Slender branches wave like hair
making ripple after ripple
shudder over the water.
A fish
   breaks
the surface.
Everything else on the river and the riverbank
   is still;
people on the bank lie in the sun;
clouds stall in the sky.
Bird and butterfly alike
   are unmoving.
Nothing stirs but
the willows.

Grammar

Agreement in sentences

Skills in tense agreement

1. Bobby refers to his current actions in the present tense.
   - Find an example of the current tense in Bobby's speech.

   'As I sit here today' is in the current tense.

2. Verbs may be in the past, present or future. Within any particular time frame, the verbs must be in the same tense.
   - Can you find a bit in the future tense?

   'We will invade your planet and kill everyone' is in the future.

3. Sometimes when verbs are abbreviated, it is more difficult to check the agreement.
   - Can you spot the abbreviated verb?

   '…he was sure he'd been abducted by aliens.'

   'He had' has been abbreviated.

Alien attack!

Bobby told me he was sure he had been abducted by aliens.

'As sure as I sit here today, I was taken to the alien ship. I had to watch a film of the future – see the world being destroyed by alien invaders – and then they set me back in my bedroom. They beamed information straight into my brain. "Tell people", the aliens said, "tell them we will invade your planet and kill everyone." No one believed me, though.'

Understanding tense agreement

We don't jump around through time, and neither should your writing! If you are writing something set in the past, you need to use the past tense consistently.

If your writing is set in the present, use the present tense.

If your writing includes speech, this might be in a different tense, but be careful to switch back to the right tense after the speech.

TRY IT OUT

Sports reports

You can report on a real or imaginary sports event for this exercise.

Write a report of a sporting event as it happens, as if you were the TV reporter giving a live commentary. Remember to write in the present tense.

Write a report of the same sports event for the newspaper. This time you are writing after the event, so it will be in the past tense.

TEST YOURSELF

Hannah and Alice was going to the shops. It is Saturday, so they could stay out all day – there was no school. Alice wants to buy some blue tights, and Hannah wanted to buy green socks. The first shop they go to were closed because it were being redecorated. The next shop is large and the girls could not find tights and socks, so they ask an assistant. 'Socks and tights, and every other type of accessory, is on the ground floor,' she says.

1. There are lots of **agreement** problems in this text. Highlight all the verbs that don't agree with their subject and underline all the verbs that are the wrong tense. Then rewrite the passage correctly.

2. Which of these sentences is correct?

   A Adrian and Bernard go to the cinema yesterday.

   B Adrian and Bernard goes to the cinema.

   C Adrian and Bernard wants to go to the cinema tomorrow.

   D Adrian and Bernard want to go the cinema.

3 Improve your skills: Reading

Punctuation is the word for the range of marks such as full stops, commas and dashes that show how to read a sentence. A punctuation test gives you the chance to show that you understand how punctuation works and that you can use it correctly.

Punctuation is as important as **grammar** in making writing make sense. It divides text into **sentences**, and inside the sentences it shows which groups of words go together and what their function is. To understand punctuation, you need to know a bit about how sentences work.

What to expect

Punctuation questions test your understanding of how punctuation works in a piece of text. They also test that you know how to use punctuation so that a reader will find it easier to understand your writing. As well as specific questions on punctuation, you will need to punctuate your own writing correctly – so you need to be able to recognise and use punctuation.

In some papers, all questions will be multiple-choice and you will need to choose the correct option to make sense of the sentence.

Punctuation skills

Punctuation is used to divide a text into sentences and to separate the **clauses** and **phrases** in a sentence. To use punctuation properly, you will need to know:

1 The parts that make up a sentence.

   Each sentence starts with a capital letter and ends with a full stop, an exclamation mark (!) or a question mark (?).

   Within a sentence, other punctuation marks are used to group words that go together and so show where to pause when reading the sentence.

2 How to identify clauses of different types in a sentence.

   Each sentence must have at least one clause. A clause has a subject and a verb.

   There are two types of clause: main clauses and subordinate clauses.

   *A **main clause** could stand alone as a sentence. A **subordinate clause** does not make sense on its own; it has a subject and a verb, but starts with a connective. It may come before, after or in the middle of a main clause. Here is an example.*

   There are no poisonous spiders in Britain,   but many British people are scared of spiders.
   Main clause   **subordinate clause**

3 How to identify **phrases** and the **parts of speech**.

   A phrase is a group of words that does not include both a subject and a verb and is not complete on its own.

The shark ate three boys,	then four fish,	then it was sick.
Main clause	phrase	subordinate clause
Makes sense alone, contains subject and verb	*no verb*	*contains connective, subject and verb*

Punctuation

Introducing punctuation

4 The different punctuation marks and how to use them.

Punctuation tells you where to pause when you read a text.

*Full stops mark the longest pauses, the pause at the end of a sentence. A comma marks a short pause. A **semi-colon** marks a pause longer than a comma but shorter than a full stop. An **ellipsis** (…) or dash (–) marks a longer pause, too.*

Read the extract, then read through the following questions and explanations.

Here are some questions you might get about this passage:

- Which group of words has mistakes in the punctuation? If there aren't any mistakes, choose X.

  A You wicked child, cried the enchantress.

  B I thought I had separated you from all the world,

  C she clutched Rapunzel's beautiful tresses,

  D the lovely braids lay on the ground.

  X There aren't any mistakes.

The speech marks are missing from the enchantress's words in A. It should say:

"You wicked child", cried the enchantress.

- How should the line *What to do I hear you say* be punctuated?

  A "What do I hear you say.

  B What do I hear you say!

  C What do I hear you say!"

  D "What do I hear you say?

  X None of the above

The sentence is a question, and it is the start of direct speech, so it should appear as "What do I hear you say? The next sentence is still part of the speech, so it doesn't have a speech mark at the end.

What you will learn

In this section you will learn these punctuation topics…

- basic punctuation
- more punctuation inside sentences.

Rapunzel

You wicked child, cried the enchantress. What do I hear you say. I thought I had separated you from all the world, and yet you have deceived me. In her anger she clutched Rapunzel's beautiful tresses, wrapped them twice round her left hand, seized a pair of scissors with the right, and snip, snap, they were cut off, and the lovely braids lay on the ground.

TIPS FOR SUCCESS
Dropping in!

- Sometimes a sentence adds a bit of extra information about something in **parenthesis**. This is a clause or phrase set apart by the punctuation. The information could be taken out of the sentence, and the sentence would still make sense.

- The extra part can be set between commas, between dashes, or between **brackets**:

  Angelica, who was head girl, found them messing about near the bike shed.

  Angelica – who was head girl – found them messing about near the bike shed.

  Angelica (who was head girl) found them messing about near the bike shed.

47

3 Improve your skills: Reading

Basic punctuation divides text into sentences and shows you when to pause while reading.

The punctuation marks you will use most are: **capital letters** and **full stops**, **commas**, **question marks** and **exclamation marks**.

Understanding basic punctuation

All **sentences** start with a capital letter, and most end with a full stop. If a sentence is a question, it ends with a question mark (?). To make a sentence into an exclamation – such as a shout – or to show that something is really surprising, you can use an exclamation mark (!) at the end.

Many sentences also have commas. These separate parts of the sentence and show you where to pause when reading.

Skills in basic punctuation

1. To show the start of a sentence, use a capital letter. To show the end of a sentence – unless it's a question or exclamation – use a full stop.
   - Highlight the start and finish of all the ordinary sentences in the passage.

     <mark>B</mark>uild a wormery and watch the worms<mark>.</mark>

     <mark>P</mark>ut soil … surface<mark>.</mark> <mark>N</mark>ext, … drop them in<mark>.</mark>
     <mark>I</mark>f … wait<mark>.</mark> <mark>W</mark>orms … wet soil<mark>.</mark>

2. A question mark shows that a sentence is a question.
   - Find the question at the beginning of the passage.

     Have you ever wondered what worms, creatures who live underground and can't be seen, do in private?

3. Commas can separate extra pieces of information that help with description. When a small piece of information is separated out and includes a **noun** and a **verb**, this is called a **subordinate clause**.
   - Can you find the subordinate clause in the first sentence?

     'creatures who live underground and can't be seen' is the subordinate clause. It can't stand on its own but the sentence works without it.

4. Exclamation marks show that something should be read with surprise or vigour. They show shouts – 'Wow!', 'Hurray!', 'Yes!' – or that something is really surprising or funny.

How to make a wormery

Have you ever wondered what worms, creatures who live underground and can't be seen, do in private? When they are far underground and no one's looking? You can find out! Build a wormery and watch the worms.

You will need a glass tank, garden soil, sand, some dead leaves – and worms!

Put soil and sand in layers in the glass tank and scatter some dead leaves on the surface. Next, collect some earthworms from the garden and drop them in. If you can't find any worms, pour some water on the ground and wait. Worms will come to the surface of the wet soil. Make sure they don't escape!

Comprehension

Read this text carefully before answering the questions below.

The stifling subway was packed, as usual. Graffiti covered the darkened windows of the trains, hiding the interior. I tucked in close to Dad and watched as the menacing crowd surged forward. The unpredictability of the mass movement was unnerving and disorienting.

'We'll wait for the next train Amy, it might be less crowded', said Dad quietly.

It was airless in the station, the lights flickered and the noise of distant machines pounded on and on. What will the creature look like? I wondered as we waited. Would it come out of its specially constructed virtual tree? How long could it survive?

It had all begun last week when Dad had come home with the evening paper…

The headline on the broadsheet was unmissable: **'Don't miss this amazing opportunity to see last squirrel'**. I *really* wanted to go. Mum had read me stories about these enchanting little creatures with feathered, furry tails. When she was little, she had loved watching them play hide and seek around the trunks and behind the boughs at the bottom of her country garden. That was before the dreadful accident. Everything was different now. The outside world was sadder and quieter: no birds, only a few wild animals, nothing left except machines and pollution. It was decided we would go on Saturday, the week had gone slowly, but now here we were waiting.

"Maybe this animal should have stayed hidden, but it will be incredible to see him", I thought.

Reading test 1

11+ English Success

Write your answers on the lines provided. When you are given a choice of answers, write the letter for the answer you think is correct, i.e. A, B, C, D or E.
Do not write answers in the 'Mark' column.

Mark

1 What was special about the squirrel?

_____

2 What was the atmosphere like in the station?
    A deserted **B** evacuated **C** organised **D** controlled **E** chaotic

3 What is meant by the word 'broadsheet'?

_____

4 Find two things from this list that can be seen from the station platform.
    1 a country garden   **A** 1 and 3 only
    2 flickering lights   **B** 2 and 4 only
    3 the noise of distant machines **C** 2 and 5 only
    4 lots of people   **D** 3 and 4 only
    5 the interior of the train   **E** 1 and 5 only

5 Why did the world seem a sadder place after the accident?

_____

6 What plants were growing at the bottom of Amy's mother's garden?
    A boughs **B** grasses **C** flowers **D** trunks **E** trees

7 How does Amy feel about going to see the squirrel?

_____

8 Why do you think Amy felt the week had gone so slowly?
    A it was hot   **B** it was winter   **C** the world was sad
    D she was impatient to see the squirrel   **E** she was bored

9 Which type of tree did the squirrel have to live in?
    A a pine tree **B** a tree trunk **C** a tree house
    D a computer-generated tree **E** a virtuous tree

10 Why is the headline in bold letters?

_____

11 Where were Amy and her father at the start of the passage?
    A at an airport **B** at a factory **C** at a power station
    D at an underground station **E** at a road underpass

12 What effect does the use of *italics* for 'really' have?

_____

© Letts Educational Ltd, *an imprint of HarperCollins Publishers*

13 What does the ellipsis (set of three dots) at the end of the fourth paragraph indicate?
   A the end of the paragraph   **B** a leap forward in time   **C** a typing error
   D a flashback in time   **E** a gap for you to fill in

14 Why does the writer use the word 'dreadful' to describe the accident?

15 How do the questions in the third paragraph help you to understand how Amy is feeling?
   A They show that she is angry.   **B** They show that she is bored.
   C They show how long it would survive.   **D** They show that she is interested.
   E They give information about the squirrel.

16 What evidence is there that the writer (Amy) likes squirrels?

17 Pick out the three adjectives that make the underground station seem threatening.
   A what, how, would   **B** surged, interior, stifling   **C** windows, trains, crowd
   D close, forward, distant   **E** menacing, airless, packed

18 Would you like to live in this world? Explain using examples from the text.

19 When do you think the passage is set?
   A last week   **B** in the past   **C** in the future   **D** next week
   E on the underground

Grammar

20 What part of speech is the word 'evening' in the phrase 'evening paper'?
   A verb   **B** adverb   **C** indefinite article   **D** pronoun   **E** adjective

21 Identify the type of the word in italics. *Graffiti* covered the darkened windows.
   A noun   **B** verb   **C** adverb   **D** adjective   **E** preposition

22 Which are the two comparatives in the last five sentences in the fifth paragraph?
   A only, slowly   **B** before, except   **C** sadder, quieter
   D no, nothing   **E** few, maybe

23 What sort of figurative language describes squirrels' tails?
   A simile   **B** metaphor   **C** assonance   **D** onomatopoeia
   E personification

24 Pick out the onomatopoeia in this new sentence.

The click, click	of Dad's shoes	on the platform	echoed the beating	of my heart.
A	**B**	**C**	**D**	**E**

25 Which word can be used to start the sentence?

Amy	Graffiti	Virtual	Softly	Hunched
A	B	C	D	E

… quietly in the corner of the carriage, the small figure couldn't see out

26 Which word can be used to start the sentence?

Reflect	Odd	Beside	Reversed	Under
A	B	C	D	E

… in the windows, strange letter patterns twisted and turned as the lights outside flicked on and off.

27 Select the correct verb to complete the sentence.

Tomorrow I

carried	will carry	carrying	have carried	carrier
A	B	C	D	E

the book to school to show my friends.

28 Select the correct verb to complete the sentence.

Years ago there

where	was	are	am	were
A	B	C	D	E

families of squirrels in many town parks and gardens.

29 Choose the correct verb to complete the sentence.

Yesterday the sky

is	will be	had been	would be	where
A	B	C	D	E

deep purple and the sun shone as the evening closed in.

30 Choose the correct verb to complete the sentence.

Amy's Dad had usually

took	take	tooken	taked	taken
A	B	C	D	E

her to the pictures on Fridays

Punctuation

31 Select the section with the missing punctuation. If they are all correct, choose X.

East Cross Station, that had been	built in 2020 was below
A	B
the city's polluted landscape and	hidden away from the devastation.
C	D	X

32 Copy this sentence, adding the correct punctuation.

the trains which dated from before the dreadful accident had torn seats rusty window frames chewing gum covered floors and a strange metallic smell

33 Copy this sentence, adding the correct punctuation.

amy pete jenny and himal had read about squirrels small tree dwelling rodents in their school natural history books

34 Select the section with the missing punctuation. If they are all correct, choose X.

The squirrel had always | loved hazelnuts they | were his absolute
A | B | C
favourite snack.
D X

35 Copy this sentence, adding the correct punctuation.

please can we take mum next time pleaded amy

36 Copy this sentence, adding the correct punctuation.

dad looked thoughtful do you think the trains will be this crowded all day he asked

Spelling

37 Which section of this text has the spelling error? If they are all correct, choose X.

There used to be monkies | with their babies | at the animal centre
A | B | C
but the accident | had created significant difficulties for the keepers.
D | E | X

38 Copy this sentence, correcting the spelling errors.

The cities were growing bigger with more peoples, more childs and more animals everywhere; even in the parkes.

11+ English Success

39. Choose the correct spelling to fill the space. If they are all correct, choose X.

It was [beter A] [bettar B] [beater C] [better D] [beatter E] [X] to catch the second train, as the first was packed with uncomfortable commuters.

40. Copy this sentence, correcting the spelling errors.

Amy thought that the squirrel looked distresed as it hoped and skiped around the strange arteficial tree.

_____

_____

41. Which section does not include a word with a prefix? If they are all correct, choose X.

Fortunately the intercity trains (A) **drowned out the mobile telephones** (B)
that were ringing (C) **with monotonous regularity.** (D) [X]

42. Add the most appropriate prefixes and suffixes to the gaps in this sentence so that it makes sense.

The carriage was _____ tidy with litter careless_____ strewn under the bench seats, which were in a state of _____ repair.

43. Pick out the correct spellings. If they are all correct, choose X.

The accident [comittee A] [committea B] [committee C] [committy D] [X] arranged for the remaining animals to be collected and placed in a virtual zoo.

44. Copy this sentence with the spelling errors corrected.

The menasing machines towered over the statoin, their ominous floresent lights flashing messeges.

_____

_____

Total (of 44)

TEST ENDS

Comprehension

Read this text carefully before answering the questions below.

The Vikings

Who were the Vikings? The Vikings, or *Norse*, were an amazing group of Scandinavian warriors who attacked Northern Europe, Eastern Asia, and Eastern North America. The exploits of the Norwegian Vikings initially led them west to invade and then trade with their western neighbours. Between 860 and 960 AD they colonised both these neighbours, Iceland and Greenland. The Swedish Vikings set out across the Baltic Sea into Northern Europe; also raiding, then buying and selling before settling in Poland, Latvia, Lithuania and Russia. By the end of the first millennium the Vikings, in their open longboats, had reached North America, five hundred years before Columbus. The word 'Viking' means one who lurks in a 'Vik' or bay and the Vikings were skilful in lying in wait before taking unsuspecting coastal villages by surprise, like sharks circling for the kill.

How do we know about the Vikings? *Archaeology* provides physical information about their daily lives, where they settled and what these settlements looked like.

The large number of horn *artefacts* found in Viking settlements led to the invention of the horned helmet by a Tudor historian, for which there is little evidence. Any Viking warrior would have known that horns on a helmet just made it easier for their opponent to grab hold of them in close battle. There is some evidence that hats with antlers were used in religious ceremonies. *Plutarch*, writing in the first century AD, describes Northern Europeans as dressing up with head-dresses that resemble wild beasts, and a ninth-century tapestry in *Oseberg*, Norway shows a man wearing a set of horns. Written recordings of the Vikings in books such as the *Anglo-Saxon Chronicle* and *Frankish and Irish Annals* were almost all written by priests. The chronicles reflect the fact that Vikings attacked their monasteries for their wealth and the accounts had a hostile tone to give a popular image of Viking atrocities. The Vikings were considered heathens for their invasions of monasteries and as a result were portrayed in the worst possible way.

What did the Vikings want to achieve? Raiding and trading provided some wealth to take back home. However, the terrain and climate of the Scandinavian countries meant that land to farm was also a desirable commodity. There were limited sources of food at home and they were interested in creating settlements in the fertile farmlands. Unlike many other invaders and settlers, they were not trying to spread their pagan religion but were keen to find out about the social and technological advances that they observed in Britain and Southern European Countries.

Did the Vikings deserve their reputation for aggression and brutality? As the only written recordings are likely to be biased and there are also many examples of Vikings trading and settling, it is possible that the Vikings were not quite the vicious villains they have been portrayed. They brought valuable commodities such as honey, tin, wheat, wool, wood, iron, fur, leather, fish and walrus ivory to the Saxons and helped build up the farming communities of Southern England. So maybe the Vikings were not quite as bad as history suggests.

Glossary

Anglo-Saxon Chronicle:	a collection of entries in Old English, with dates, recording the history of the Anglo-Saxons
archaeology:	study of ancient cultures through their remains
artefacts:	objects made by human beings, especially those that have archaeological or cultural interest
Frankish and Irish Annals:	descriptive accounts recording the activities of the seafaring tribes during the times of the Vikings
Oseberg:	town in Norway
Plutarch:	Roman writer and historian, born 46 AD
Norse:	relating to ancient or medieval Scandinavia, or its people or culture

11+ English Success

Reading test 2

Write your answers on the line provided unless instructed otherwise. When you are given a choice of answers, write the letter for the answer you think is correct, i.e. A, B, C, D or E. *Do not write answers in the 'Mark' column.*

Mark

1 Which countries were the western neighbours to the Viking homelands?

   _____

2 Which area of water did the Swedish Vikings cross when they first started raiding?
   A North Sea   B Atlantic Ocean   C English Channel   D Baltic Sea
   E River Thames

3 Which of these words is closest in meaning to the word 'climate'?
   A mountain   B weather   C fjords   D colonised   E circling

4 Why were the Vikings different from other invaders and settlers?
   A They came from the North.   B They sailed in boats.
   C They didn't try to spread their religion.   D They were pagan.
   E They wore helmets.

5 Find two things that were traded by the Vikings.
   1 books   A 1 and 5 only
   2 sharks   B 2 and 4 only
   3 fur   C 2 and 3 only
   4 food   D 3 and 4 only
   5 religion   E 3 and 5 only

6 Who first wrote about the Vikings wearing head-dresses?

   _____

7 Why might the Anglo-Saxon writings be biased?

   _____

8 If Columbus discovered America in 1482, approximately when did the Vikings discover America?
   A 1432 AD   B 1982 AD   C 982 BC   D 500 AD   E 982 AD

9 Why do you think the many written recordings about the Vikings were made by priests?
   A Priests were the only people interested in the Vikings.
   B Priests were the main group of people that could read and write.
   C They only worked on Sundays so they had a lot of time to complete chronicles and books.
   D The other people who recorded information had their recordings destroyed.

10 Why does each paragraph start with a question?

    _____

© Letts Educational Ltd, *an imprint of HarperCollins Publishers*

Reading test 2

11+ English Success

11 What is the second paragraph about?
  A Viking warriors   B Viking farming   C What we know about the Vikings
  D The Chronicles   E The Norwegian tapestries

12 How are different typefaces (bold and italic) used to help the reader?
  _____

13 Choose another heading that could be used for the final paragraph.
  Did the Vikings deserve their reputation for aggression and brutality?
  A Who were the Vikings?   B How long ago did the Vikings live?
  C Viking daily life   D Friend or foe?   E Viking Gods

14 What do you think 'commodity' means in paragraph 3?
  A something funny   B rapid movement   C products
  D house   E church

15 Why do you think the writer calls the written records 'Chronicles'?
  _____

16 What does the writer suggest that the Vikings helped to set up in the South of England?
  _____

17 What positive things did the Vikings bring to Britain?
  A They brought valuable articles to trade.
  B They made the Saxons follow their religion.
  C They taught the Saxons about their Gods.
  D They brought boats to sell.   E They destroyed the churches.

18 What evidence is there that the Vikings could have had some hats with horns?
  _____

19 Where might you find this text?
  A In a natural history book.   B In a fiction book.   C In a poetry book.
  D In a science fiction book.   E In an encyclopedia.

Grammar

20 The *exploits* of the Norwegian Vikings initially lead them west to raid and trade with their western neighbours.
  What part of speech is the word *exploits* in the above sentence?
  A verb   B noun   C pronoun   D adverb   E preposition

21. There is some evidence that hats *with* antlers were used in religious ceremonies.
    What part of speech is the word *with* in the sentence above?
    A verb   B noun   C possessive pronoun   D preposition
    E definite article

22. The word 'Viking' means one who *lurks* in a 'Vik' or bay.
    What part of speech is the word *lurks* in this sentence?
    A adjective   B possessive pronoun   C preposition
    D definite article   E verb

23. What sort of language technique has the author used when calling the Vikings 'vicious villains' in the final paragraph?
    A onomatopoeia   B alliteration   C metaphor
    D simile   E personification

24. Look at the last line of paragraph 1. What sort of language technique is used to describe how the Vikings gathered in the bays?
    A metaphor   B personification   C onomatopoeia
    D simile   E assonance

Choose the word that will fit best at the beginning of these sentences.
Write the letter for the answer you think is correct on the lines provided.

25. … by the sword was supposed to be the Viking's way of communicating with the Saxons.
    A Quickly   B Under   C Negotiation   D Equals   E Full

26. … Scandinavian artefacts like oval brooches, whalebone plaques and ornate swords hilts have been found throughout the South of England, showing evidence of trading.
    A Typical   B Type   C Like   D Rapidly   E They

27. Circle a verb from each of the pairs so that the text makes sense and the verbs agree.
    Can you *build/built* a ship, *cross/crossing* the seas, *looted/loot* a monastery and *return/returning* home to claim your prize?

28. Circle a verb from each of the pairs so that the text makes sense and the verbs agree.
    Extensive excavations at the Coppergate, York, have *provide/provided* us with a good *understand/understanding* of what Jorvik (York) *would have/will have* been like at the time when Eric the Viking *rules/ruled* over the city.

29. Choose the best pair of words to complete the sentence.
    So many Vikings … settling in Britain, place names … to Viking names.
    A were, change   B is, changes   C were, changed
    D is, changed   E where, changed

30. Which two words fit in the spaces to complete this passage?
    Bjorn …… not care whether any Saxons …… killed or injured.
    A do, is   B does, is   C do, are   D does, are   E do, be

Punctuation

31 Pick out the section with the punctuation error in it. If they are all correct, choose X.

Their swift wooden longships | equipped with both sails and oars, | enabled
A | B |

them to mount piratical raids | on the settlements of the British Isles. | X
D | E |

32 Rewrite the sentence with the punctuation corrected.

the brother and sister frey and freyja the god and goddess of fertility were also important and there were many other minor gods and goddesses

_____

_____

33 Rewrite the sentence with the punctuation corrected.

viking children had wooden dolls played football sailed model boats and played horn trumpets

_____

34 Pick out the section with the punctuation error. If they are all correct, choose X.

"Sailors and settlers," | laughed Brother Francis, | more like greedy plunderers
A | B | C

that sneak up and steal your treasure." | X
D |

35 Pick out the section with the punctuation error. If they are all correct, choose X.

There is one thing | you need to know about | Vikings they weren't
A | B | C

popular with the Saxon priests. | X
D |

36 Rewrite the sentence below, correcting any punctuation errors.

king alfred pray to your god and wait to see what happens because the viking guthruns coming with all his mates

_____

_____

Spelling

37 Pick out the section with **no** spelling errors. If they are all correct, choose X.

I showed off all my jewellery, | rings, broochs and bangles, | and the witchs
A | B | C

told storys while they laughed at me. | X
D |

38 Copy the sentence below, correcting any spelling errors.

Wolves, bears and sheep were the animals we knew best in our home countries.

39 Choose the option in which all three words are spelt correctly to complete the sentence.

The ... Viking had blood ... from his ...

A terrible, dribbling, dager   B terible, dribling, dagger
C terrible, dribbling, dagger   D terible, dribling, dager
E terible, dribbling, dager

40 Copy the sentence with the spelling errors corrected.

The Saxon farmer was spliting logs and striping the bark from the strong young saplings.

41 Copy the sentence filling in the gaps with the missing prefixes or suffixes.

The Saxons were ...arranging and clear... their village longhouse after the ...expect... raid by the Vikings.

42 Circle the correct prefix from each pair to complete the sentence.

The Saxons were *dis/un* organised and *un/dis* prepared for the sudden raid on the *un/ex* protected coastline.

43 Choose the answer option with the correct spelling to fill the gaps.

The Viking boys were ... to carry a knife with which they could cut ... meat.

A allowed, there   B aloud, their   C allowed, they're
D allowed, their   E aloud, there

44 Copy the sentence with the spelling errors corrected.

The Vikings loved to practice there rowing skills and sang mischivous songs about their freinds and enenmies.

Total (of 44)

TEST ENDS

11+ English Success

Dictation

Do not read this passage before taking this test. The test is not timed.

Ask somebody to read out the text slowly in short sections, leaving time for you to write it down.

What's Floating Over London?

The latest form of transport being considered for our inner cities is the hovercraft.

This amazing machine, first built in the 1950s, can travel over different surfaces. This means that bursting tyres on potholes will be a thing of the past.

The London Mayor is very keen on this idea and has already planned a competition to find the best logo to decorate the hover fleet. The race is on.

"Send us your most inventive plans," urges the scheme's new Project Manager.

Spelling

Do not look at the words before taking this test. The test is not timed.

Ask somebody to read out the words – repeating each word twice and leaving time for you to write it down.

A	pad	ten	fig	got	but
	any	you	why	talk	true
B	trot	grim	rush	them	silk
	view	bird	each	early	final
C	clear	slice	liar	mouse	weave
	bright	should	awful	busy	juice
D	island	once	friend	Wednesday	February
	feather	exciting	quite	tomb	unruly
E	referred	questionnaire	interview	vicious	useable
	cemetery	secretary	schedule	sincerely	serviceable

Dictation

Do not read this passage before taking this test. The test is not timed.

Ask somebody to read out the text slowly in short sections, leaving time for you to write it down.

It was late. There were shadows on the wall. A candle stood on the dining table, its light reflected in the mirror hanging over the fireplace. Photographs were arranged on the window ledge with a plant that looked rather tired.
"When is Pete getting home?" asked Hannah, looking at the clock.
"I'm not sure," replied her Mum, trying to sound calm and unconcerned.
First there had been the sound of an explosion and then the power cut.
Could it all be linked?

Spelling

Do not look at the words before taking this test. The test is not timed.

Ask somebody to read out the words – repeating each word twice and leaving time for you to write it down.

A	bit	cat	get	lot	put
	the	one	was	are	they
B	this	chin	most	left	band
	said	four	who	again	next
C	tape	chair	house	share	east
	light	could	until	enough	many
D	people	before	settle	limit	size
	laugh	quiet	comb	truly	written
E	disappear	business	introduction	medicine	vehicle
	choir	orchestra	necessary	parliament	advertisement

Writing tasks

11+ English Success

Choose your writing task from the following selection. You should allow 45 minutes to complete this. The asterisks show which are the most difficult tasks and relate to the second task you will choose after completing your 11+ practice.

Fiction

Story

1. Complete the story using the story opener:
   'They knew something was wrong the moment they opened the door...' *
2. Write a story that ends with, '...and it turned to powder as they watched.' **
3. The Unfortunate Accident *
4. The Day the Gorilla Came to Stay *
5. Grandma's Roller Skates Go Missing *
6. The Haunted Castle *
7. The Search for the Ruby Crown **
8. Bank Robber Lane **

Playscript

9. Write a scene from a play called 'Into the Dungeon'. *
10. Write a scene from a play set in the spacecraft control centre, with the title 'Mission to Mars'. **

Non-fiction

Discussion text

11. School should start at 6.00am and end at 6.00pm. Discuss. *
12. Should children give half their pocket money to charity? Discuss. **

Explanatory text

13. Imagine you have been given an unusual pet from outer space. Make up an explanatory text so others know all about the pet and how to look after it. *
14. Imagine you have been given a skateboard that hovers. Make up an explanatory text to tell your friends about how to fly it. **

Instructional and procedural text

15. Write a recipe for a 'Perfect Parent'. **
16. Write an instruction sheet for 'How to make a trap to catch live beetles'. *

Non-chronological report

17. Write a report about your favourite game. *
18. Write a report on an ideal destination. **

Persuasive writing

19. Write a radio advertisement for a new breakfast snack. *
20. Write a persuasive text to explain how giving children more power would help the country. **

Recounts

21. *A week in the life of...* Choose a creature or character and write about their week in diary form. *
22. Write an explanation of how you lost your homework. **

Letter writing

23. Write a letter to your local newspaper describing the sighting of a rare animal/bird/insect in your area. *
24. Write a letter of complaint about the closure of the local adventure playground. **

Punctuation

Basic punctuation

- There are three sentences in the text with exclamation marks. See if you can find them.

  'You can find out!' is one example. However, an exclamation is not always a proper sentence; it can be a single word or a response to a question, such as 'Eeeeek!' or 'No way!'

- Look at the last sentence in the text: 'Make sure they don't escape!' Think about why the sentence has an exclamation mark.

  The exclamation mark has been used here to lighten the tone, making the sentence surprising and amusing (because it makes you think of the worms wriggling out). It makes the instruction sound less bossy.

5 Commas are used to separate **clauses**, **phrases**, **adjectives** and items in a list. A subordinate clause that comes in the middle of a sentence has a comma before and after it.

- Find a sentence that uses commas to separate items in a list.

  You will need a glass tank, garden soil, sand, some dead leaves – and worms!

TIPS FOR SUCCESS
Comma sense

- Putting commas in the wrong place can completely change the sense of what you write.
- For example, 'Laura is pretty, musical and sporty' means that she is pretty and musical and sporty; 'Laura is pretty musical and sporty' means that she is quite musical and sporty.

TRY IT OUT
Take a breather

- Practise your speaking skills by reading out a passage from a favourite magazine to a friend or your family.
- Every time you see a comma, pause for the length of time it takes to say 'ten' in your head.
- Every time you see a full-stop, pause for the length of time it takes to say 'hundred' in your head.

TEST YOURSELF

Gabrielle closed the door and sat on the bed it was gloomy, but she was sure she saw something out of the corner of her eye could there be someone in the room she didn't want to turn the light on – just in case there was she tried to calm her nerves but she had only been there a minute when she heard something rustle softly there was someone – or something – there what was it she heard it wasn't quite rustling it was more muffled it entered her head that it was a noise of feathers a bird a bird must have got trapped in her room she sighed with relief and turned on the light there was no bird beside the wardrobe stood – could it be yes unbelievably – an angel

1 Divide the text into sentences. You can use three question marks and three exclamation marks, and as many commas, full stops and capital letters as you need.

2 Which of these is a proper sentence? If none is, choose **X**.

   A At about half-past three,

   B It was yellow and very smelly.

   C while the ghost was walking around the castle

   D Falling off the cliff.

   X None of them.

More about punctuation

3 Improve your skills: Reading

Punctuation within a sentence shows how words are grouped together.

Punctuation such as **commas**, **colons** and **semi-colons** help you make sense of a text.

Understanding more about punctuation

Punctuation within a **sentence** breaks up the sentence into smaller units of sense. It shows you where to pause when reading a text, and how words work together.

TIPS FOR SUCCESS
Apostrophes

An **apostrophe** can be used to show that a letter has been missed out.

Goats don't mind what they eat.

- A **possessive apostrophe** can also be used to show something belongs to somebody or something.

  The goat's field was next to the railway line.

  The goats' field was next to the river.

- When the apostrophe is before the 's' there is only one goat, when it is after the 's' there is more than one goat.

Skills in additional punctuation

1. **Speech marks** tell you where the words that are spoken or thought by a character begin and end. Only use speech marks if you are writing *exactly* the words that someone said or thought.

   - Which words in this **paragraph** form the question that Robinson Crusoe asked himself?

     "How shall I keep my goats out of the way of enemies?" You can tell these are the exact words because they begin and end with speech marks.

Keeping goats

The next question to answer was, "How shall I keep my goats out of the way of enemies?" This is the plan that I made: I would fence in three or four pastures far away from one another, and well hidden by trees; then I would divide my flock, so that if one pasture were found by them, the others might be safe.

***Robinson Crusoe**, by Daniel Defoe*

2. A colon (:) introduces a list, an explanation, or sometimes a speech.

   'This is the plan that I made: I would fence in three or four pastures…'
   The colon introduces the plan that Robinson Crusoe explains.

3. A comma (,) marks a short pause in a sentence. It separates **adjectives**, items in a list, or **clauses**. A clause is a group of words that includes a **subject** and **verb**. There are two types of clause: a **main clause** makes sense on its own; a **subordinate clause** needs to be attached to a main clause to make sense.

   - Find an example where commas are used between two clauses. Which part of the sentence makes sense on its own?

     'I would fence in three or four pastures far away from one another, and well hidden by trees.' The first part makes sense on its own; the second part doesn't.

4. **Dashes** are used either side of a part of the sentence that you want to set apart from the rest. A dash sets words apart more than commas but less than **brackets**. You can also use a dash rather a like a colon, to show that something follows on from what goes before, or to add a pause. Dashes can make your writing quite jerky.

   Robinson Crusoe has been stranded on an island – will he escape alive?

Punctuation

More about punctuation

5 An **ellipsis** (…) is used to show that something has been missed out, or to show passing time or thoughts.

Robinson Crusoe thought for a while… He would build a shelter!

Understanding semi-colons

A **semi-colon** (;) marks a longer pause in a sentence. The part that comes after the semi-colon is often an explanation of the part before, or it may be the next item in a sequence.

A semi-colon is also used to link related clauses, such as: 'Alice liked cats; her favourites were fluffy ginger cats.' Often, the semi-colon could be replaced by a **connective**: 'Alice liked cats, and her favourites were fluffy ginger cats.'

The semi-colon is sometimes used to break up the action: '…I would fence in three or four pastures far away from one another, and well hidden by trees; then I would divide my flock…' First, Crusoe will fence off his pastures, then divide his flock of goats.

Semi-colons often separate items in a list if each item is several words long, like this: 'He bought three green balloons; a red and yellow flag; two chickens and a water pistol.'

TRY IT OUT

Move it!

Find a passage of text with a variety of punctuation marks, such as those listed on this page (you can use the passage in the 'Test yourself' questions below once you have completed question 1).

- Choose a different action for each punctuation mark, for example: shrug for a question mark, lift your arms for an exclamation mark, nod for a comma, jump for a colon.
- Now read it out to a friend and see if they can guess the punctuation marks as you read through the passage.
- You can read it again with your friend and try to speed up your reading – doing the actions together.

TEST YOURSELF

Most of the punctuation has been taken out of this passage of text.

We packed some snacks to take in the boat sandwiches apples cakes lemonade and crisps. Hattie wanted to take bananas but I said they'd get squashed. She grumbled and started to sulk. Shut up Dan said. Hattie started to cry the trip was going wrong already. Here Hattie I said why don't you find a picnic blanket And some sweets they won't get squashed.

1 Correct the punctuation in the passage. You need to use these punctuation marks, in this order:

: , , , , " ! " ; " , , " , " ? ; "

2 Which of these sentences is correctly punctuated?

A The farmer grew cauliflowers in one field, potatoes in another; and cabbages in his best field.

B Cars and motorbikes sped past the dog, he didn't know which way to go.

C Egyptian plovers are plucky birds; they clean the teeth of Nile crocodiles by going into the croc's mouth – it's a dangerous job!

D Ticks are hideous parasites that suck the blood – like vampires, of a host animal.

X None of them.

Introducing spelling

3 Improve your skills: Reading

Good spelling is important as it helps people to understand your writing.

There are a lot of spelling rules to help you learn to spell, and some words are – helpfully – written just as they sound.

What to expect

In the test there are likely to be questions about spelling and you will also need to show that you can spell correctly in your own writing.

Spelling questions might ask you to spot or correct spelling mistakes in a piece of writing, or to choose the right spellings. The challenges include forming plurals correctly, choosing the right **homophone** (a word that sounds the same as another word), using **suffixes** and **prefixes**, using tricky groups of letters, and working out when you need to double a letter.

This is the type of question you might get about the passage below:

1   Which of these sentences has a spelling mistake?

   A   The wolf cub crept threw the trees

   B   A mouse scuttled in and then out again

   C   That just made the den seem even emptier

   D   A pitiful, long howl that echoed around the hollow.

   *Answer A has a spelling mistake: 'threw' is a **homonym**, and the word which should have been used is 'through'.*

Spelling skills

Types of letters

1   **Vowel** sounds can be long or short. This just tells you whether they are slow or quick to say. Here are some examples:

Vowel	Long vowel sound	Short vowel sound
a	rain, grape, late	pan, hat, happen
e	keep, lean, wheel	wet, send, crept
i	hide, ripe, line	till, spit, fin
o	stone, boat, grow	dog, not, bob

The sound gives you a clue about how the word is spelt. A word with a long vowel usually has two vowels – either together or separated by one **consonant**.

Words

1   Spelling is important to reading and writing. You need to know how to spell for your own writing, but you also need to be able to work out how to say new words you come across in your reading.

  • Some words are made up from smaller words – breadboard, dustbin and seagull are examples.

   Often, you can work out what a word means if you know how it sounds.

The wolf cub crept threw the trees to the den, expecting to find his brothers and sisters snuggled inside. But the den was cold and empty. Where could they be? A mouse scuttled in and then out again – that just made the den seem even emptier. A pitiful, long howl echoed around the hollow.

Spelling

Introducing spelling

2. Some words are easy to work out by sounding out the letters, especially when you know about the odd groups like 'th', 'ch' and 'sh', which have their own special sounds.
   - Some words that are easy to work out are: thatch, church, shift.

     Because these words contain the special sounds, these words are easy to spell, even if you have not seen them before. However, sounds don't tell you how to say or spell all words. English is a bit trickier than that.

3. You've probably learned a lot of spelling rules already, such as how to use magic 'e' and how to sound two vowels together (like 'oo' or 'ea'). There are other simple rules to help you work out spellings, but there are also some words that break the rules and you just have to remember how to spell them.

'The llama adores hyacinths but the ptarmigan abhors them.'

Skills in syllables and stresses
Syllables
Words are made up of **syllables**.

A syllable is a group of letters that forms a single unit of sound.

1. Some words have just one syllable.
   - Examples are: mum, dog, hen, car, girl, boat, snake and zoo.
2. Lots of words have two syllables.
   - Examples are: donkey, measles, football, bottle, magic.

     You can break these into two parts that you can say separately.
3. Some longer words have three syllables.
   - Examples are: antelope, tangerine, computer, pyramid.
4. Some words have four…or even more!
   - Examples are: helicopter, transformative.

Stresses
When a word has more than one syllable, it usually has a stronger **stress** on one or two syllables than on the others.

A stress is when a syllable is said with more force than the others in the word.
   - Say these words and phrases to see how it works. The strong stresses are highlighted:

     fish finger; ca**the**dral; **kan**garoo; bal**loon**; **tor**toise; **salt** and **vin**egar.

What you will learn
In this section you will learn about these spelling topics…
- forming plurals using spelling rules
- when to use double letters
- how to use prefixes and suffixes to make new words
- dealing with tricky spellings.

TIPS FOR SUCCESS
Tackling spelling
- The more you read, the better your spelling will become. Reading helps you to learn spelling without really trying – the words become familiar and you use them easily.
- It's a good idea to keep a list of spellings you find tricky. Write them down and try to learn them – using a word helps you to learn it. You can add new words to the list as you come across them.
- A good way of learning the spellings of new words is to look at the word, say it aloud, then cover it up and see if you can write it correctly. If you get it wrong, try again.

53

Plurals and spelling rules

3 Improve your skills: Reading

English has quite a few tricky plurals, but luckily there are rules to help you remember them or work them out.

Nouns are words for things, people and ideas. When you write about two or more things, you need to use a **plural** form of the noun. There are different ways of forming plurals.

Understanding plurals

By following some simple rules, you can make most nouns plural – but there are a few unusual ones that you just have to learn.

For many words, you form a plural just by adding 's' after the **singular** form of the noun (the form used for just one thing). For example: one dog, two dog**s**.

For other words, there are rules that help you work out the plurals.

A few words have unusual plurals that you just have to remember. For example: one child, two child**ren**; one person, two pe**ople**; one head l**ouse**, two head l**ice**; one t**oo**th, two t**ee**th.

Skills in making plurals

1   For most words, you just add an 's' to make a plural.

- Look at the animals fed at 12:00. The plurals for all these names work in this way.

   penguin**s**   seal**s**   tiger**s**

2   If the word ends with a 'y' ('but not with 'ey', 'ay', 'oy', 'uy'), you need to throw away the 'y' and use 'ies' to make the plural, as in these examples.

   one fair**y**   two fair**ies**

   If the word ends with 'ey', you just add 's', as usual:

   one donke**y**   two donke**ys**

- The animals fed at 1:00 follow these spelling rules.

   Bush bab**ies**   monke**ys**   wallab**ies**

3   If a word ends 'ess', 'ch', 'th', 'sh' or 'x' you need to add 'es' to make the plural:

   one godd**ess**   two godd**esses**
   one wat**ch**   two wat**ches**
   one fo**x**   two fox**es**

   Some words that end with 'o' take 'es' as well:

   tomato**es**   hero**es**

Zoo rules

Please note that some of the animals are dangerous. In the petting zoo, you may feed the cow, the sheep, the cat, the donkey and the mouse.

In the main part of the zoo you may not feed the animals but you can watch at feeding times.

Animals are fed at the following times:

   12:00   Penguin, seal, tiger
   12:30   Ostrich, lioness, hippo
   1:00   Bush baby, monkey, wallaby
   1:30   Wolf, calf

Spelling

Plurals and spelling rules

…but some take just 's' (for example, pianos).
The animals fed at 12:30 all follow these spelling rules.

ostrich**es**   lion**esses**   hippo**s**

4 Some words are the same in the singular and the plural:

one sheep   two sheep

one deer   two deer

Most types of fish are the same in the singular and plural, too: one cod, two cod; one salmon, two salmon; one plaice, two plaice.

5 Many words that end with 'f' change to 'v' and add 'es' to make the plural.

- The animals fed at 1:30 both follow these spelling rules.

wol**ves**   cal**ves**

6 There are some plurals that are quite different from the singular words: words ending in 'ouse' mostly change to 'ice'. Look at the animals in the petting zoo and see if you can change these all to plurals.

cow   sheep   cat   donkey   mouse

'Mouse' changes to 'mice' because it ends in 'ouse'. But be careful – this doesn't apply to all 'ouse' words: the plural of 'house' is 'houses'. It is a good idea to look up words like these in a dictionary to see how their plurals are spelt.

7 The same rules apply to **verbs** that take an 's' – so 'I watch' but 'he watches'; 'I miss' but 'she misses'; 'we apply' but 'it applies'.

TIPS FOR SUCCESS

Plurals and adjectives

- When the name of something includes an **adjective** and a **noun** – like 'head louse' – only the noun changes when you make the plural.

    Head lice

TRY IT OUT

Collecting plurals

Spot plurals in everything you read for a day and make a note of them. You might find them on notices, on packaging, in books and magazines, in adverts and shops.

- Make a list, putting them into groups by how the plural is formed.

TEST YOURSELF

Brigit would have liked camping better if there had not been so many mosquitos. They bit her arms and legs and even her eyes lids, near her lashs. She liked everything else – cooking potatoes in the embers of the camp fire, toasting marshmallows and flicking matchs into the fire – but the best thing of all was watching the monkies swing in the trees.

1 Which one of these plurals is correctly spelt?

   A mosquitos

   B eyelashs

   C potatoes

   D matchs

   E monkies

2 Write the passage out again, correcting all the spelling mistakes.

Doubling letters

3 Improve your skills: Reading

Sometimes, words need repeated (doubled) letters to be spelt correctly.

Vowels before and after double letters, generally have short sound. By doubling letters in some words you can keep the sound of a word the same when you are changing its ending.

Understanding doubling

The way words sound depends on the sequence of letters. Magic 'e' changes the way we say the vowel sound in a word. So, the short 'a' in 'cap' doesn't sound the same as the long 'a' in 'cape'. Magic 'i' might do this, too. To stop a magic 'e' or 'i' making **verbs** sound wrong, we double a letter to keep the 'i' or 'e' far enough away from an earlier vowel so that it can't work its magic!

Sophie *hops* in the playground.

Sophie is *hopping* in the playground.

Sophie *hopped* in the playground.

Without doubling, 'Sophie would be *hoping* in the playground', which would mean she 'hopes' for something.

The following words all follow this rule; the extra **consonant** helps the sound to stay the same. Compare the sound of the words with and without the double consonant:

pin/pining/pinning; scrap/scraping/scrapping; star/staring/starring

Skills in doubling letters

1 To work out if a verb uses doubling, try saying it in a **sentence** with 'I' – such as 'I sip tea'. Does the word end with a vowel (a, e, i, o, u) and one consonant (other letter) – as it does in 'sip'? If so, you probably need to double the last letter. But look out – if a word ends with 'w' or 'y' (such as 'bow' or 'play') you never double it.

- Highlight all the verbs in the passage. Which verbs follow the same pattern as 'sip', ending with a single vowel and then a single consonant? Write out all these verbs, adding 'ing' to the end.

Playing nicely

Please be nice in the playground and follow these rules to keep everyone happy and safe.

- Don't skip, jump or run in the areas marked for special games.
- Don't trip anyone up on purpose.
- Don't slap, bite or hit anyone.
- Only throw or kick balls in the red area.
- Play any very lively games in the red area.
- If you want to sit quietly, go to the blue area.

Following, skipping, running, tripping, slapping, hitting, throwing, playing, sitting.

Spelling

Doubling letters

2. If the verb ends with 'e', you don't need to double the last letter, you just drop the 'e' before adding 'ing' or 'ed' – so 'I place', 'I am placing', 'I placed'.
   - Find a verb in the passage that ends with 'e' and write it with 'ing'.
   *Bite, biting. Look out – the past **tense** of 'bite' is not 'bited' but 'bit'.*

3. If the verb ends with more than one consonant together, you don't need to double the last letter.
   - Find the verbs that end with two consonants and add 'ing' and 'ed'.
   Jump, jumping, jumped; marked, marking; kick, kicking, kicked; want, wanting, wanted.

4. If the verb has two vowels together before the last consonant, you don't double the last letter: 'look', 'looking', 'looked'.

5. If you are just adding an 's', you don't need to double the last letter. Only double a letter if adding 'ed' or 'ing'.
   - Add 's' to these verbs from the passage: skip, jump, run, trip, slap, bite, hit.
   Skips, jumps, runs, trips, slaps, bites, hits.

6. If a word ends in 'er' you sometimes double the 'r' and sometimes not when adding 'ing' or 'ed'. If the main stress of the word is on the last **syllable**, you double the 'r' – so 'prefer' becomes 'preferring' and 'preferred' but 'bother' becomes 'bothering' and 'bothered'.
   - Add 'ing' to these words: 'occur', 'whisper', 'infer'.
   Occurring, whispering, inferring.

7. Sometimes you have to use doubling when making a **noun**; the rules are the same. For instance – 'bedding' goes on a 'bed', and 'leggings' go on a 'leg'. You might even have to use doubling to make an adjective: something that makes you 'mad' is 'maddening'.

8. Words that end in 'le' often have a double consonant before the 'le': 'bottle', 'wiggle', 'puddle'.

9. If a vowel sound is short, there is often a double letter before or after it: 'rubbish', 'wedding', 'sparrow'.

TRY IT OUT

Ribbon rows

Make a collection of words with double letters.

- Make a card for each word and write the double letters in a different colour so that they stand out.
- Put holes in the corners and thread them onto a ri**bb**on. You can put two beads between each card if you like.
- Add to your doubles ribbon as you 'collect' new words and hang it up so you can see it everyday.

TEST YOURSELF

We hope you will enjoy your stay in the hotel. If you want to swim in the pool, please ask for a towel in reception. Follow the safety guidelines to have fun. Please do not endanger yourself or others.

1. Change all the verbs in the passage to 'ing' endings.
2. Which of these verbs is wrongly spelt?
   - **A** gurgle – gurgling
   - **B** whip – whipping
   - **C** free – freeing
   - **D** feel – feelling
   - **E** spot – spotting

Prefixes and suffixes

3 Improve your skills: Reading

Prefixes are groups of letters added to the front of a word to change its meaning. Suffixes are groups of letters added to the end of a word.

Common **prefixes** include 'pre-', 'anti-' and 'un-'.

Common **suffixes** include '-ly', '-er' and '-ful'.

Understanding prefixes and suffixes

Prefixes and suffixes are groups of letters that can be attached to other words to change their meaning in the same way each time. For example, the prefix 'un' turns a word into its opposite. 'Uncomfortable' is the opposite of 'comfortable' and 'unnecessary' is the opposite of 'necessary'.

Skills in using prefixes and suffixes

1. A prefix comes at the start of a word. It doesn't matter if you end up with a doubled letter when you add a prefix – so when you add 'un' to 'necessary', you get 'unnecessary'. Don't miss out the extra 'n'!
   - Find four words with prefixes in the passage and highlight the prefix.
     *Un*comfortable, *dis*agree, *anti*social, *un*friendly.

2. Sometimes, if the word starts with a **vowel** and the prefix ends with a vowel, the word can look a bit odd and may be hard to read: '*co*operate', '*micro*organism', '*pre*eminent'. If you think it could be confusing, you can use a **hyphen** after the prefix, for example '*re*-enter', '*co*-opt'.

3. Common prefixes are: 'dis' (not), 'un' (not), 'pre' (before), 're' (again),
   'sub' (under), 'mini' (small), 'micro' (very small), 'non' (not).
   - Add a prefix to each of these words to make another word:
     marine; beast; suitable; satisfied; recorded; cycle; scope.
     *Sub*marine, *mini*beast, *un*suitable, *dis*satisfied, *pre*recorded; *re*cycle; *micro*scope

4. A suffix is added to the end of a word to change its meaning. The suffix 'ly' is added to make an **adverb** from an **adjective** – as in slow/slow*ly*. The suffix 'tion' turns a **verb** into a **noun** – as in inhibit/inhibit*ion*. The suffixes 'er' and 'est' are used to show comparison, as in 'fast', 'fast*er*', 'fast*est*'. If the word ends with the same letter as the start of the suffix, double the letter, unless it's 'e'. So you get beautiful/beautiful*ly*, but late/lat*er*.
   - Find four words in the passage with different suffixes and highlight the suffix.
     Love*liest*; quick*ly*; fruit*less*; tall*er*/rich*er*.

Henry and Maria

Maria was beautiful and Henry was uncomfortable in her presence. He thought she was the loveliest girl he had ever seen, and hoped she would quickly become his friend. They spent hours talking, but he was afraid to disagree with her and scared of looking antisocial or unfriendly if he did. His attempts to win her attention were fruitless, though. Maria was in love with someone else – the taller, richer microbiologist Edgar.

Spelling

Prefixes and suffixes

5. If a word ends with 'y', change it to 'i' when adding a suffix: 'pretty'/'prettiest'.
6. Common suffixes are 'ed', 'able', 'tion', 'ly', 'less', 'ful', 'est'. If a word ends in 'e' and the suffix starts with a vowel, drop the 'e' at the end of the word: create/creation. If the word ends in double 'e' ('ee') you need to keep both of them (unless the suffix starts with 'e'): agree/agreeable, but 'agreed'.

   - Add a suffix to each of these words to make another word:
     quick; comfort; small; beauty; accommodate; home.
     Quickly; comfortable; smallest; beautiful; accommodation; homeless.

7. If removing the 'e' means the word would be spelt the same as a different word, you may need to keep the 'e': so 'dye' (to change the colour of something with a dye) becomes 'dyeing', because 'dying' means 'becoming dead'.
8. Sometimes you need to make extra changes to the end of a word when adding a suffix.
9. Sometimes different prefixes or suffixes can be added to the same word '**root**'. For example, cycle can become bicycle, unicycle or recycle. Care can become careful, caring, carefully or careless.

TRY IT OUT

Word webs
Choose a word that has a prefix or suffix and write it down in the centre of a page. Then think of other words with the same prefix or a suffix, writing them around the word, joining them to the original word with a line. Think of other words with prefixes and suffixes to join to your new words to make a word web.
For example…

- Prefix: *tele*graph – *auto*graph – *auto*mobile
- Suffix: home*less* – home*ly* – love*ly*

See how big you can make it grow!

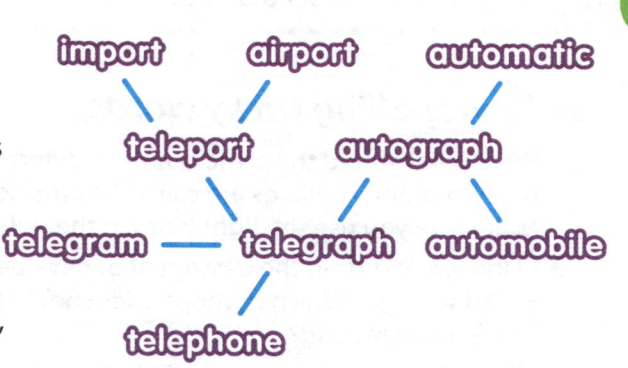

import — airport — automatic
teleport — autograph
telegram — telegraph — automobile
telephone

TEST YOURSELF

Sometimes I go to school on my cycle and then I go past the market. The market is full of interesting people, sights and sounds. On the way home, I like to cycle clockwise around the market, then park my bike and find a corner where I can sit in comfort and watch what is happening. If it's a hot day, I sit and read in the shade of a tree. I like to read fiction best of all. Some stories have a happy ending, but I don't like those very much.

1. Pick out words from the passage that can take a prefix and write them in the table. The first one has been done for you.

bi	un	anti	dis	non	super
bicycle					

2. Which of these groups of words with prefixes and suffixes includes a spelling mistake?

   A disease, disservice, disturb   B quickly, faithfuly, happily

   C unwilling, unlikely, unstable   D inflammable, inedible, incapable

   X None of them.

Tricky spellings

3 Improve your skills: Reading

English has lots of rather odd spellings. You can learn spelling rules to help you. However, there are some words that don't fit the rules, so you just have to remember them!

Some strange groups of letters crop up again and again, and sounding out words can help. Some words have letters you don't sound, though – look out for silent letters.

Understanding tricky spellings

Some basic rules like this can help you work out some spellings:

*'When two **vowels** go walking, the first vowel does the talking'* – this helps you to spell or read words like 'b**ea**k' and 'b**oa**t' (make the sound of the first vowel when two come together).

There are also groups of letters that commonly appear together that you will soon recognise – like 'ght' and 'tion' or 'sion'.

Some words that are hard to spell don't fit rules and you just need to remember that they are a bit odd.

Skills in spelling tricky words

1. Words that sound the same but have different meanings and spellings are called **homophones**. Make sure you use the right word in the right place.
   - Find two words in the passage that have been used wrongly. Which homophones should have been used instead?

   The neighbour hadn't 'scene' Craig, but this should be 'seen'.

   The description says Craig has 'white hare' – it should be 'white hair'.

2. If a 'g' or 'c' is followed by 'e', 'i', or 'y' it has a 'soft' sound like 'j' or 's'. A hard 'g' is the 'g' sound in 'hog'; a soft 'g' is the sound in 'gentle'. The word 'cat' has a hard 'c', and the word 'mice' has a soft 'c'. If there are two 'c's in a row, there may be both sounds: 'accident' has a hard 'c' and a soft 'c'.
   - Find a word in the passage that has a hard and a soft 'g'.

   'Garage' has a hard 'g' at the start and a soft 'g' at the end. The hard 'g' is followed by an 'a' and the soft 'g' by an 'e'.

3. Look out for common letter groups such as 'ght', 'tion'/'sion', 'tch', 'tious'/'cious'. These groups aren't sounded out in the way that they are written.

Gone missing

It was a rainy day when I noticed Craig wasn't there any more. I searched in the shrubbery and behind the garage; I hunted through the rhododendron bushes and amongst the poppies. But he wasn't there. I knocked on the neighbour's door, but woman next door hadn't scene him. I made this sign and put it near the light at the end of the drive:

Gone: Gnome

Description: tubby; blue trousers; furry hat; white beard; white hare

Height: 70cm

I won Craig in a competition; I hope he comes back.

Spelling

Tricky spellings

- Find some words that share a group of letters that don't sound as they are written.

  The words 'neighbour', 'height', and 'light' all have a 'gh' group that is not sounded.

4 Some words have silent letters, such 'knob', 'gnome' and 'autumn'.

- Find three words in the passage with a silent letter.

  These words have silent letters: rhododendron, knocked, neighbour, light, gnome, white.

5 The group 'ur', 'ir' and 'er' all have the same sound 'er': 'hurt', 'dirty', 'her'.

- Find a word in the passage that has an 'er' sound but is spelt differently.

  'Furry' has an 'er' sound.

TIPS FOR SUCCESS
Homophones
People often mix up these homophones – make sure you use them in the right places:

- here (in this place) and hear (perceive sound)
- there (in that place), they're (they are) and their (belonging to them)
- too (more than enough), to (towards) and two (2)
- your (belonging to you) and you're (you are)
- its (belonging to it) and it's (it is).

TRY IT OUT
Cartoon capers
Try to find some long words that contain the letters of shorter words, for example dedi**cate**.

Write your words at the top of separate cards then highlight each shorter word within the longer word: dedi**cate**, sep**ara**te (a rat), **pi**geon, phl**eg**m, ant**enn**ae, envi**ron**ment.

Now draw cartoons of the words you have found on the cards.

Come up with new rules for difficult words such as 'c**ommittee**'. All the double letters show there are many people on a committee.

TEST YOURSELF

Our science field trip to the pond was very hare-raising. We sore lots of mini-beasts in the water, but that's knot all that happened. Pedro rode across the pond in a boat, but he took the wrong root and got stuck in the reads. The son was very bright, and he was stuck four too ours before Mr Williams noticed and through a rope to him. He tide the rope to a peace of would at the front of the boat and Mr Williams helped pull him to the sure. Annabelle was stung by a be, and Katie was throne in the water by some bad buoys. We aren't aloud to go on any moor school trips in the currant year.

1 There are lots of mistakes in this report on a school trip. All the words are correct spellings, but the wrong homophones are used. Highlight all the words that are wrong and give the right words.

2 Which of these groups of words includes a spelling mistake?

    A knee, knife, gnaw, write

    B cautious, anxious, suspicious

    C kitchen, witch, attach, church

    D edge, sandwidge, fudge

    X None of them.

3 Improve your skills: Writing

Creative writing tasks give you an opportunity to have fun with language, demonstrate your writing skills and create interesting, imaginative texts.

You might be asked to write a play, a poem, a story, or part of a story. Although you are making up your piece, you still need to be careful about your writing, including spelling and **grammar**.

What to expect

You may need to write or continue a story, a play or even a poem. You will also be expected to show that you can create or follow a plot, make up characters and a setting. Your choice of language should make your descriptions seem real and put across both the feelings of the characters and the atmosphere of the place you are writing about. Consider who is going to read it and choose your language to match.

Understanding creative writing

When you write a story, a play, or perhaps a poem, you need to think about the plot, the characters, the setting and the voice that tells the reader what is happening.

The **plot** is the storyline – it's what happens in your piece of writing.

Characters are the people who take part in the story or play.

The **setting** is where your story, play or poem takes place.

Dialogue is the words your characters speak.

The **narrator** is the person or voice that tells the story. It can be someone in the story, called a first-person narrator, who appears in the story as 'I', for example: 'I took my rabbit for a walk.' Alternatively, the story can be told by a third-person narrator who refers to the people in the story, for example: 'Mrs Bumble took her rabbit for a walk.'

Skills in creative writing

Structure

1 You must write a story in proper sentences and paragraphs.

   A paragraph is a group of sentences that link together a series of points or ideas.

   In a story, a paragraph often deals with what happens to a character at a particular time, or shows one episode in a story. If you start talking about a different character, place or time, then start a new paragraph.

2 Use connective words and phrases to make your writing read naturally.

   Connectives and phrases convey time, move attention to different characters or places and create excitement!

   When you are planning your writing, it is worth writing down some useful connectives and phrases that could be used in your story. Some useful connectives are: 'later', 'in the morning', 'outside', 'suddenly'. Some useful phrases are, 'at that moment', 'just then'.

Fiction, plays and poetry

3 Make sure you stick to the same tense.

   A story follows a series of events logically and can move around in time.

   Stories can be set in the past or present tense. Whichever you pick, use the same one throughout for the narrative – though when characters speak, they may use different tenses.

Style

1 Your choice of words will have a major impact on the style of your piece of writing.

   Your words should be adventurous, imaginative and relevant to your choice of genre.

   Developing a focused vocabulary is something that you can do with practice. Have fun making lists of different words you can use for colours, e.g. green, emerald, lime, sea, sage, verdigris, grassy, jade, olive, leaf, pea.
   This helps you think around a word so that you can avoid repeating the same descriptions.

2 The length and structure of the sentences can vary the pace and hold the reader's interest.

   Sentences should start in different ways and be of varying length.

   Lots of short sentences make a choppy, fast-paced style that is good for an exciting, tense scene. Long sentences full of descriptive words make a slow pace, and can build up tension in a spooky story.

3 The pictures and comparisons you make will encourage your audience to enjoy your writing.

   Use a variety of descriptive techniques to build the reality of your text.

   Adjectives, **adverbs**, **metaphors**, **similes**, **personification**, **onomatopoeia** and **assonance** can be used to bring your descriptions to life. You can make the same physical setting very different by describing it in different ways. If your story is set in a castle, it could be very dark and scary, or it could be bright and cheerful, full of colour and lively people jousting, dancing and feasting. Make sure your descriptions suit the type of story you are writing.

Breaking rules in plays and poems

1 In real life, people don't always speak in whole sentences.

   Dialogue often uses fragments of sentences.

   If someone is scared, in a hurry, or excited they may speak in a jerky way, with lots of very short sentences or phrases, or even single words, like this…

   Laurence: 'No! Not in there! Don't, Abby – it's too dangerous!'

2 Poems are very rarely written using complete sentences.

   Poems often have words ordered in different and unusual ways.

TIPS FOR SUCCESS

Who, when, where, why, what, how?

- Ask yourself these questions to help you plan your story, play or poem:
- Who is it about?
- When is it set?
- Where is it set?
- Why is the action happening?
- What happens?
- How does it happen?

What you will learn

In this section you will learn these creative writing skills…

- writing stories
- writing plays
- writing poems.

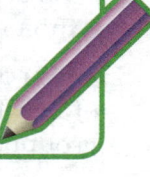

3 Improve your skills: Writing

Writing stories

A good story draws readers in so that they want to find out what happens.

To make your own stories exciting, you need to think about the characters, the story line, the writing style and the 'shape' of the story.

Understanding story-writing

A story must have a carefully crafted shape, interesting characters and a good setting. The writing style must suit the story, too. There's a lot to think about.

There are different types of stories, such as mysteries, science fiction and funny stories. Look at 'Different styles of fiction writing' on pages 76–77 to find out a bit about the different types.

To make sure your story really works, it's a good idea to plan it before you start. Make sure you know what is going to happen, what the characters are like, and how they act with each other.

Skills in writing stories

1 A story must have three main parts:
- a beginning, in which you set out the characters, setting and subject matter
- a middle, where the events build and complications appear
- an ending, which shows what happens and ties up any loose ends.

Work out the plot before you start and make sure it follows this structure.

One small step...

Lia put her foot down. She was used to the weightless feeling, as her training and her time in space had prepared her for that. She didn't know whether she would feel dust or rock, though, and was surprised to bounce. Ever since she had stepped on the moon, Lia had dreamed of being the first to step on a new planet, somewhere else no-one had ever been.

'Hey! Todd!' she called into his helmet microphone. 'It's bouncy! C'mon on out here!'

It was only then that she saw the line of red flesh that snaked across the ground towards her foot.

Fiction, plays and poetry

Writing stories

- The first **paragraph** gives you an idea about what a story will be like. What do you expect from this story? What kind of story is it?

  The story will probably show us where Lia is and what the planet is like.

2. For a plot to be exciting, there must be some mystery or problem that the characters have to solve. A story in which everything goes smoothly is not interesting – readers like to see people struggle! A mystery or exciting event draws readers into your story.

   - Can you see a mystery or problem lined up for this story?

     The 'line of red flesh' is a mystery at this point. We want to read on to find out what it is and what it will do.

3. Work out where and when your story takes place and make it clear to your readers.

   - Where does this story take place? Does that lead you to expect a particular type of story? *It takes place on another planet, which leads us to expect a science fiction story.*

TIPS FOR SUCCESS

Tell me a story

- Before writing a story it's a good idea to decide who will tell your story – a **third-person** narrator or a **first-person** narrator ('I')?

- The first two **sentences** of this story have been rewritten using a first-person narrator.

  I put my foot down. I was used to the weightless feeling, as my training and my time in space had prepared me for that.

4. It's a good idea to write a description of each character in your story, things like their name, age, job, what they look like, and what they are like as a person – kind, cowardly, mean? Bear all their characteristics in mind as you write, and choose words that suit them.

   - What do you think the character Lia is like?

     She is an astronaut, someone who likes adventure; she's curious and excited by what is happening to her.

5. Dialogue gives you a good chance to show what your characters are like. Make sure the dialogue fits in with the way you want them to appear – so if you have a grumpy character, don't have them say 'Hi! What a beautiful day!'

   - From the way Lia speaks, do you think you will like her?

     She wants to share the experience with Todd, and speaks in an informal, friendly way that seems to show the author wants us to like her.

Writing plays

3 Improve your skills: Writing

Playscripts are made up almost entirely of dialogue – the words people say to each other.

However, a play is designed to be performed, not just to be read, so you need to think about what your characters do on stage as well as what they say.

Understanding how to write plays

Plays have a **cast** of **characters** who interact largely through **dialogue** and actions. There is only direct speech in a play – the words the characters say. Although there are no narrative passages, you can use **stage directions** to describe actions and events that should happen on stage.

Playscripts can be for performance on stage, for filming, audio recording, making an animation on a computer or to be shown as a cartoon strip.

Look at 'Different styles of fiction writing' on pages 76–77 to give you ideas about some different types of plays.

Skills in writing plays

1. Plan the **plot** of your play by writing a list of what happens and who is involved at each stage. List the characters (the cast) and work out what they are like. Remember that what they are like must come across in their speech.

   - In the play extract on the right, think about who the cast is. Which is the character worried about hygiene? Which character likes the house to be tidy?

     The cast is Daddy bear, Mummy bear and Baby bear. Daddy bear is concerned with hygiene – he hopes no one has licked his spoon. Mummy bear doesn't like the mess.

2. Introduce each character's words by giving their name, followed by a **colon** (:). Start each speech on a new line. Don't add 'said' or any other narrative.

3. Plays are often divided into scenes that take place at different times and often in different places. Each scene starts with a line saying where and when it happens. For example:

   Scene 3: The bears' house, late morning

4. Use stage directions to tell the actors what they are to do on the stage, and also to describe the scene. Think about how stage directions are used in this extract.

   The stage directions tell the actor playing Baby bear to start crying, and tell the actor playing Mummy bear to put an arm around him.

Bears with porridge

Scene 3

The bears' house, late morning

DADDY BEAR: Someone's been eating my porridge! How disgusting! I hope they didn't lick the spoon.

MUMMY BEAR: Someone's been eating my porridge! They spilt some on the table – what a mess!

BABY BEAR: Someone's been eating my porridge – and they've eaten it all up! [bursts into tears]

MUMMY BEAR [putting an arm around Baby bear]: There, there, darling. I'll make some more. Sit in your chair – Oh! Look at the chairs!

Fiction, plays and poetry

Writing poems

Poems come in lots of different forms. All poems try to make a reader look at their subject in a new way.

Writing poems is very different from writing prose. Poetry uses language to create powerful and often surprising effects.

Understanding poetry

Writing a poem gives you the chance to play with language. You can use sound patterns, exciting words and **figurative language** to share your ideas and make your reader see the world in the way you see it.

Poems can be descriptions, they can be sad or happy, funny or serious. There are many different types of poem (see page 77) but you can also make up your own patterns for poems. A poem is very personal.

The tiger

Tiger, tiger, burning bright
In the forests of the night,
What immortal hand or eye
Could frame thy fearful symmetry?

From **The Tiger**, by William Blake

Skills in writing poems

1. You can use **rhyme**, **rhythm**, repetition, **alliteration**, **assonance**, **onomatopoeia** and other effects to create sound patterns. You need to count syllables and stresses to work with rhythm.

   - These highlighted sections pick out the strong stresses in the first two lines of the poem. Highlight the stresses in the rest of the poem. What do you notice? Which lines rhyme?

   Tiger, tiger, **burning** **bright**

   In the **forests** **of** the **night**,

   The repeating pattern of strong/weak/strong/weak stresses creates a steady rhythm. Lines 1 and 2 rhyme with each other, and lines 3 and 4 rhyme with each other.

2. Use **imagery**, such as **metaphors** and **similes**, to help readers see what you are describing in a new way. Use striking and unexpected images that suit the subject of your poem.

   - Why do you think Blake says the tiger is 'burning bright'?

   The word burning makes us think of fire, and the orange flames are the colour of the tiger. It's a way of making us see the tiger's colour, but also brings the associations of fire: that it's exciting and dangerous.

3. Use your imagination and put words together in any way that helps to make a picture or feeling for the reader.

   - What does this line make you think of?

   Bibble, bobble, bubble – over every pebble.

   It's about water – and sounds like water bubbling over stones in a stream.

Introducing non-fiction writing

3 Improve your skills: Writing

Non-fiction is any type of writing that presents facts or opinions rather than something that is made up. These tasks give you the chance to demonstrate your writing skills to produce a text that is suitable for its purpose.

Non-fiction writing includes reports, recounts, letters, discussions, instructions and explanatory texts. These are written in different ways and have different aims.

What to expect

Each non-fiction writing task will tell you the type of writing you have to produce. You will be marked on how well you match your writing to the usual conventions and style, as well as on your content and general writing skills. You might be asked to write a personal piece, such as a letter to a friend, or perhaps a report for your school.

TIPS FOR SUCCESS
Perfect planning
- Write in whole sentences, divided into paragraphs, and use suitable **connectives** to make your writing flow smoothly.
- Use a suitable style for your **audience**. You wouldn't write a letter to your parents in the same way as you write a report for a newspaper, for example.
- Check your spelling and **grammar** carefully when you have finished.

Non-fiction writing skills

When you approach a non-fiction writing exercise, begin by planning what you will write and how you will organise it. Make sure that you know…

1. The sort of writing that is being asked for. It could be…
   - a formal letter
   - a descriptive piece
   - a recount.

   Deciding on the genre you are writing in will help you to structure your ideas across to match your chosen style.

2. What the topic is. It might be…
   - something you already have information about
   - something you will need to invent, but in a specific non-fiction genre.

   Read the question carefully and make notes of any facts that you already know that will help you plan your work. You will lose marks if you write about the wrong thing.

3. How you will structure your writing.
   - Does it need an introduction?
   - Does it need a conclusion?

   In most writing tasks you will need an introduction, followed by the main part of your writing, which should develop or expand the points you want to make, and finally a brief paragraph to sum up or add a conclusion.

What you will learn

In this section you will learn how to write these types of non-fiction…
- discussion pieces
- explanatory texts
- instructional texts
- non-chronological reports
- persuasive writing
- recounts
- letters.

Non-fiction

Writing discussion texts

A discussion text is about an issue that can be viewed in more than one way.

It gives a balanced account and does not try to persuade the reader that one view is right.

Understanding discussion texts

A discussion text begins with an introduction that explains what the topic is. The rest of the piece gives different views about the topic, but doesn't say one is right and others are wrong. Discussion texts are often about issues people feel strongly about, such as whether we should eat meat. You need to set your own beliefs aside when writing a discussion text.

Skills in writing discussion texts

1 In the first **paragraph** of a discussion text you need to set out the issue that you will discuss. Explain the topic, but give only facts, not your views on the issue.

- This discussion topic is about smoking and personal choice. An introduction at the beginning helps to make the topic clear.

   Should smoking be banned? Or is it up to individuals whether they choose to take the risks involved in smoking? There are arguments for both views.

2 In the following paragraphs, present different views about the issue. In each case, give all the arguments for one view, with evidence to back them up, and all the arguments for the other view, again with evidence. Write about the same amount on each view, and deal with points in the same order in each section.

No smoking?

… Even so, many smokers say the choice is theirs: as long as they have been given fair and accurate information about the dangers of smoking, they say, it's up to them if they want to take the risks. Usually, we trust people to make their own choices about risky activities and smoking should not be different.

- What do you think the opposite view to that in the passage would be?

   The opposite view is that smoking should be banned or discouraged.

3 Use **connectives** between **sentences** within each paragraph and to introduce the opposite view. Words such as 'however', 'but', 'although' and phrases like 'even so' and 'on the other hand' will help you to do this.

- How can you tell this passage follows a paragraph giving the opposite view?

   It starts with 'Even so', a phrase you would use to introduce a different point of view.

4 In your last paragraph, summarise the two views. If the evidence for one is much stronger than for the other, you can say this, but don't say 'I think…'. Remember that it's not a personal piece.

69

3 Improve your skills: Writing

Explanatory texts explain how something works or what happens in certain circumstances or events.

You might need to write an explanatory text about a scientific topic, or about something that happens now or has happened in the past.

Understanding explanatory texts

When you write an explanation, you must aim to write as clearly as possible. Don't give your own **opinions** or thoughts about the topic – just the facts.

Watching an eclipse

An eclipse happens when the moon passes between the Earth and the sun, hiding all or part of the sun. In a total solar eclipse, it becomes dark in the middle of the day. It's exciting to watch an eclipse, but it's important to do so safely.

In the first stage of the eclipse, the moon covers part of the sun. As it moves, more and more of the sun is covered. 'Totality' is when just a ring of the sun's light is visible around the edge of the moon.

Skills in writing explanatory texts

1. Start an explanatory text with one or two **sentences** that introduce the topic.
   - What will this text be about?
     It will be about how to watch an eclipse safely.

2. Explain the topic using separate sentences for each part of the explanation. Use **connectives** to link the parts of the explanation. If one thing causes another, use connectives such as 'because' or 'so'. If things happen in a certain order, use time connectives such as 'then' and 'afterwards'.
   - Can you spot the connectives used in this passage?
     'But', 'In the first stage', 'As'.

3. Write your explanation in the present **tense** unless it is about something that has happened in the past and does not happen any more.
   '…the moon covers part of the sun. As it moves…'

   If you are writing about a historical event, use the past tense all the way through.
   'When there was a banquet in the great hall, the kitchens were hot and steamy and the servants turning the spits would be running with sweat…'

4. Write in an impersonal style, in the **third person**. You probably won't be writing about individuals, but about groups.
   'It's exciting to watch an eclipse, but it's important to do so safely.'

   If this were a more personal and informal piece, it could have said 'Watching the eclipse will be exciting, but you must do it safely.'

5. Give the steps of your explanation in a logical order and stop when you get to the end. Write a sentence to sum up, if that suits your topic.

Non-fiction

Instructional and procedural texts

An instructional text tells readers how to do something. It is presented as a set of directions or steps to follow.

When you write an instructional text, giving clear details in the right order is the most important task.

Understanding how to write instructional texts

Instructions are addressed to a person who is going to follow them. For this reason, they are written in the **imperative** voice – this means a style of writing that tells someone what to do. 'Shut up!' is an imperative; so is 'Put the dish on the table.'

Skills in writing instructional texts

1. Start your instructional text with a short **paragraph** saying what the instructions are for. For example, to make a cake; fix a puncture in a bike tyre; or clean a rabbit hutch.
   - Begin by considering what the text is about.

     This text is about keeping vampires away from your room while you sleep.

2. List any equipment needed before you start the instructions.
   - Think about the best way to present your list.

     Go through the process you are going to write about and list all the items that will be needed before you begin, then check the list after you have finished writing. This text lists equipment in the 'You will need:' list.

3. Make each stage a separate paragraph.
   - Decide if it matters which order these instructions are carried out in before you begin.

     *If the steps have to be covered in a particular order, you can number the steps. If they can be followed in any order, use **bullet points** instead of numbers. Put the most important points first if they don't have to be done in order.*

     This text is not a sequence, but a set of things to do.

4. Be precise where necessary. This may mean giving exact quantities or using **adjectives** and **adverbs**.
   - Look for an example of this from the passage. How could this have been more precise? Would that be appropriate?

     It suggests using 'five or six' cloves of garlic. It also says to scatter 'many' rice grains. It would not be appropriate to specify how many as a number, but it could give the weight of rice to use.

5. Sometimes it is useful to draw a quick diagram to help explain things.

Vampire-proof your room

Vampires visit in the night to suck your blood. If you live in an area where vampires are a problem, this is how to protect yourself.

You will need: garlic, rice, a cross and silver jewellery (such as a ring or necklace).

What to do:

- Put five or six garlic cloves around each of the windows and doors to your room. Vampires don't like garlic.
- Scatter many rice grains over the threshold. Vampires have to stop and count all the grains before they can cross.
- Hang a cross over your bed. Vampires can't approach a cross.
- Wear some silver jewellery. Silver repels vampires.

Non-chronological reports

3 Improve your skills: Writing

A non-chronological report deals with a topic that is not organised by time.

This type of report explains a **subject**, giving factual and sometimes technical information in a logical order.

Understanding reports

Chronological means 'relating to time'. Something that is reported in chronological order is told in the order in which it happened. A non-chronological report deals with a topic that has nothing to do with time – such as how engines work or how animals adapt to living in the desert. As the report can't be ordered in a sequence, you need to find some other logical way to structure it.

Dinosaurs in the hen-house

The birds that are found in every country of the world today are all distantly related to the dinosaurs that roamed the Earth 65 million years ago. Although dinosaurs were reptiles, their direct descendants are birds.

Scientists, using different types of evidence, have shown that birds are closely related to dinosaurs.

Skills in writing reports

1. Start your report with a **paragraph** that introduces the topic and states what you will write about.
   - What is this report going to be about?
     It will be about the fact that birds have developed from dinosaurs.

2. Use the **third person** (describe things or people as 'it' or 'they'), rather than the **first person** ('I', 'you' or 'we').
   - Look at how the text appears more formal when this **sentence** is changed from the first person to the third person:
     'We may think of all dinosaurs as very large.'
     'Many people think all dinosaurs were very large.'

3. Use comparison and description to give information, not to create special effects or **imagery**. Don't write about specific 'characters' but about the general group of people, animals or objects you are discussing.
   - Think about how the line below can be rewritten to make it more suitable for a report:
     'Tragically, all the poor dinosaurs were killed by a terrifying disaster 65 million years ago.'
   - Removing the emotional language means it reads more formally:
     'All the dinosaurs were killed by a major disaster 65 million years ago.'

4. Organise your report into paragraphs that deal with different aspects of the topic, arranged in a logical order and using **connectives** to join them. You may need to include technical information and perhaps some diagrams, graphs or pictures.

Non-fiction

Persuasive writing

A persuasive piece tries to convince the reader to share the writer's point of view.

Advertisements and **propaganda** use persuasive writing. They may try to flatter you, appeal to your common sense, or present a case it is difficult to disagree with.

Understanding persuasive writing

When you write a persuasive piece, you don't need to give both sides of an argument. Instead, give as much evidence as you can to support your own view. If you mention an opposing view, it should be to criticise or discredit it.

Pay me – I'm working!

Children should be paid to go to school.

- Adults who go to school are paid: teachers, cleaners and dinner ladies all take home a salary. This shows that their work is valued. Children work harder than anyone else in a school, so their work should be valued, too – it's only fair!
- School work is a preparation for later working life. Clearly, it would be more like working life if children were paid for what they do.
- Paying children would improve attendance.

Skills in writing persuasively

1. Begin with a statement of the position you are going to promote. You will usually start with quite a general statement and write about more specific aspects later on.
2. Write in the present **tense**, not about individuals but about groups of people or things.
   - Look for the groups of people mentioned in the passage.

     Children, adults, teachers, cleaners and dinner ladies.
3. Present a series of points in support of your position, giving evidence or arguments to back them up. You might use **bullet points** to identify each point.
4. Use **connectives** that stress the logic of your case, such as 'so', 'therefore', 'because', 'it follows that'. Try to make it difficult for the reader to disagree with you.
   - Find some connectives used in the passage to make it look as though one point naturally leads to the conclusion that children should be paid.

     'This shows…', 'so…', 'clearly…'.
5. You can use emotive language, or try to manipulate the reader using phases like 'it's only fair!' or 'it would disappointing if…'
6. End the piece of writing by restating what you want the reader to believe.
   - Consider a suitable ending for this passage.

     Children should be paid to attend school, reflecting the value of what they do and the fact that they are the workers of the future.

Recount texts

3 Improve your skills: Writing

A recount text gives an account of something that has happened in the past.

It tells in **chronological** order the stages of an action or event. It might be about something that happened to you personally or about a historical event

Understanding recounts

A **recount** is always written in the past **tense**. If you are writing about something you experienced or saw yourself, use the **first person** ('I ran along the road'). If it happened to someone else, or is an event from history, use the **third person** ('The soldier hid in the trench').

The baby bird

Last spring, my sister and I found a baby bird that had fallen out of its nest and we looked after it.

We found the bird lying on the path in the garden. We couldn't see a nest, or a parent bird. The baby was very cold and we thought it would die, so my sister gently picked it up and we took it into the house.

Then inside, I made a warm nest from a curled up sock in a box. Next, we put the bird in the nest and put our tortoise's heat lamp nearby to shine into the box and keep the bird warm.

Later that day, we found some worms to feed the bird.

Skills in writing recount texts

1. Start your recount with an introduction that sets the scene and explains what you are writing about and when it happened.
   - Look at the first **paragraph** to see how it introduces the recount.
     It clearly outlines that the writer and her sister found a baby bird and looked after it the previous spring.

2. Write in the **first person** or **third person** about specific people and a specific event. For example…
   'I made a warm nest…'

3. Tell the events in the order they happened. Don't jump backwards and forwards through time to make the story more exciting – but you can add details and descriptive words to make your recount livelier.

4. Use **connectives** that show how time passes, and to show how one stage causes another, if appropriate.
   - Look at how the connectives used in this passage show how time moves on.
     'Then', 'next', 'later that day'.

5. End with a closing comment that sums up the experience.
   - Write a possible ending to this recount (you can make up any details you need). For example…
     The three weeks we spent looking after the baby bird were hard work, but really good fun. When the bird flew away, we were both happy and sad at the same time.

Non-fiction

Letter writing

**People write letters for lots of reasons.
Letters can be formal or informal.**

You might want to rewrite an informal letter to a friend or a member of your family, full of gossip and news. You may need to write a formal letter to a newspaper, to the council or a business.

Understanding letter-writing

When you write a letter, you need to decide whether it is formal or informal. You have much more freedom in an informal letter to someone you know than in a formal letter. Write all letters using proper **sentences** and **paragraphs**. However, the style, opening, ending and what you write in the letter will vary depending on who you are writing to.

> 15 Basildon Terrace,
> Little Whining
> Norfolk
> NR36 6WW
>
> Missing jumper
>
> Dear Mr Gardener
>
> Last week, I rented a boat from Gardener's Boats when I was on a school trip.
>
> Unfortunately, I think I left my blue school jumper under the seat in the boat, as I can't find it. I live a long way from the boating lake so I can't come to pick it up.
>
> I would be grateful if you would you please look for the jumper and post it to me at the address above if you find it.
>
> Yours sincerely
>
> Harry Bond

Letter-writing skills

1. Start a letter with 'Dear' and then the name of the person. In a formal letter, use 'Dear Mr …' or 'Dear Mrs …' If you don't know the person's name, write 'Dear Sir/Madam'.
   - Look at the letter to decide whether it is formal or informal.
     This is a formal letter; it starts 'Dear Mr Gardener'.

2. Set out clearly what your letter is about and divide it into paragraphs that introduce the letter, explain the **subject** and then sum up what you expect or want next. This is especially important in a formal letter; an informal letter may be chattier and less organised. Start a new sentence for every new piece of information and use polite, **formal language**.
   - Read through the letter again to see what happens in each paragraph.
     *The first paragraph says that Harry has been to the boating lake, and when that was.
     The second explains that he has left his jumper in the boat, and what it looks like.
     The last paragraph asks the owner of the boatyard to send it back to him.*

3. End a formal letter with 'Yours sincerely' if you have used the person's name or 'Yours faithfully' if you have used 'Dear Sir/Madam'. In an informal letter, you can end with something more relaxed, such as 'Best wishes' or 'Lots of love'.

3 Improve your skills: English essentials

Different styles of fiction writing

Creative writing questions may ask you to write in a specific genre or form. You need to know a little about each of these so that you can write in the correct way.

You may also be asked to write a letter about an imaginary subject.

Stories and plays

There are many types of story. Those you are most likely to come across or be asked to write or continue are…

- adventure
- mystery
- historical fiction
- science fiction
- fantasy
- contemporary fiction
- dilemma stories
- myth.

All of these types of writing can also be used when writing plays. Here are a few things to remember when writing each type.

Adventure

Adventure stories have an exciting plot, usually followed in **chronological** order without flashbacks (telling previous incidents). They build excitement through surprise and tension as the reader tries to work out what will happen and how problems will be resolved. Slow down the telling to create tension, and speed it up to make an exciting pace. The characters are usually people we can feel strongly about, liking the hero or disliking the villain. A surprise ending is good!

Mystery

Mystery stories have to keep a reader guessing. Reveal details slowly, and create a spooky or mysterious atmosphere. Asking **rhetorical questions** is a good way of increasing the sense of mystery – 'What could that eerie scratching noise be?' Use **adjectives** and **adverbs** to create a feeling of mystery or fear, and show your characters being puzzled or afraid. Mystery stories are often (but not always) set in spooky places such as dark forests, old castles, empty buildings or other deserted, dark areas.

Historical fiction

Historical stories are set in the past. You will need to create a realistic historical setting, so make sure you don't include any details that don't fit the time – Romans didn't have mobile phones! You can use real historical events and add extra events and characters that you make up. Sometimes, historical stories start at a later point in time, with a character remembering what has happened and the story following in flashback.

Science fiction

Science fiction is usually set in the future, sometimes on a different planet. It usually includes lots of details about the way people live, special machines and technologies that might exist in the future, and even aliens from space. Science fiction gives you the chance to let your imagination run free – but don't forget that it still needs a proper storyline and characters. Something exciting has to happen, it can't all be descriptions of monsters and machines! You will need to use description carefully so that readers can imagine your new world.

English Essentials

Different styles of fiction writing

Fantasy
Fantasy stories, like science fiction, use imagined places that are unlike the normal world. Description and **imagery** are important so that your readers can visualise the setting. You still need an exciting plot and characters. The telling may be chronological, but some fantasy and science fiction stories include time travel. If you use this, keep careful track of when things are happening so that your readers don't get confused.

Contemporary fiction
Contemporary stories are those set in the present day. They use familiar settings and characters who are like real, modern people. You will need to use realistic dialogue, including the informal way children speak to each other as well as the way adults talk, and how children and adults talk to each other – but you don't need to write down *everything* that is said. You will need less description than you do in a historical, fantasy or science fiction story, as many parts of the setting will be familiar to your readers.

Dilemma stories
A dilemma story focuses on a character's difficult choice. Introduce the dilemma early on, and add to the tension and difficulty by complicating matters and not allowing an easy answer. Characterisation is really important in a dilemma story, as the main 'action' takes place in the character's mind. Use dialogue, description and action to show what your characters are like.

Myths and legends
Myths are often larger-than-life stories of heroes and villains or monsters. They may involve dangerous journeys, lots of adventures, monsters, fights and people with super-human powers. Use description and **imagery** to make your story vivid, keep it moving quickly and draw strong characters. Myths generally don't include much dialogue.

Poems
Poems come in many different forms. Some are very long, and others are very short. Some rhyme, and some don't. The types of poem you might be asked to write in an exam are…

Structured poems
- haiku – three lines with 5, 7 and 5 syllables, not rhyming
- cinquain – five lines with variable patterns of syllables, but often 2, 4, 6, 8, 2, not rhyming
- kenning – a poem that describes something without saying what it is. It has short lines that each gives a feature of the thing or person. Kennings don't usually rhyme.
- rap – a chanted rhyme that often runs quickly and makes unusual and lively rhymes. It often uses informal 'street' language.
- limerick – a funny poem with a syllable pattern 8, 8, 6, 6, 8 and a rhyming scheme a, a, b, b, a.

Free verse
A poetic description or account of something that does not have to use rhyme or syllable counts but varies line length, sound patterns and stresses to create an effect.

Visual poems
Visual poems include calligrams, shape poems and concrete poems. This style of poem is where its shape has an important part in creating the overall effect.

3 Improve your skills: English essentials

abbreviation	a short version of a word or group of words, e.g. rhino (rhinoceros)
acronym	an abbreviation of a group of words to make a new word, using just the initial letters, e.g. laser (light amplification by the stimulated emission of radiation)
active	where something or someone is doing something, e.g. The bird pecked Liz.
adjective	a word that describes a noun, e.g. blue flowers
adverb	a word that gives extra meaning to a verb, e.g. She ran quickly along the path that led to the woods.
alliteration	where each word starts with the same letter or sound, creating an effective image, e.g. one wiggling worm; seven silent cygnets
anecdote	a short, often amusing, personal account of an incident or event
antonym	a word with an opposite meaning to another word, e.g. hot – cold, happy – sad, black – white
apostrophe	a punctuation mark that indicates either missing letters or possession, e.g. you'll, Leah's puppy
article	a word that goes with a noun to show what it specifies, it can be definite or indefinite. a definite article, e.g. this, the an indefinite article, e.g. a, an
assonance	the similarity or repetition of two or more vowel sounds, especially in words that are close together in a poem, e.g. The wind sings in the valley.
asterisk	a punctuation mark that refers the reader to footnotes below the text, or replaces letters in words that are rude or inappropriate, e.g 'Run like h*ll!' shouted Peter.
audience	the people who read a writer's books or other writing
bold print	darker print that **stands out** and is therefore easily noticed
brackets	a punctuation mark that is used to enclose an explanatory word or comment and separate it from the main sentence, e.g. Sophie ate up the cabbage (though she hated it).
bullet points	marks that tell the reader they are reading a list or linked points
capital letter	a letter in its larger format that is used to begin sentences and start proper nouns, e.g. The cat runs into the room. His name is Charlie.
chronological	text written in time order
clause	a group of words that expresses an event, e.g. Sunil is happy; Mia makes dinner.
cliché	an over-used phrase or opinion, e.g. red as a rose; My brother eats like a pig.
colon	a punctuation mark used to introduce a list or a following example, e.g. Sarah bought three things: a cake, a pizza and a jar of pickles.
comma	a punctuation mark used to help the reader by separating parts of a sentence. It sometimes indicates a short pause in speech, e.g. The girl, who had black curls, walked to the hairdressers.
comparative	compares a characteristic of one thing to that of another. Comparatives include bigger, higher, quieter
complex sentence	a sentence consisting of a main clause, which itself includes one or more subordinate clauses, e.g. The underground station, crowded with commuters, had an unusual smell and strange lights that flickered on and off.
compound word	a word made up of two other words, e.g. football, headrest

English essentials

Glossary

conditional	a conditional sentence is one in which one thing depends upon another. May contain the conjunction 'if', e.g. I'll come tomorrow if the sun shines.
conjunction	a word used to link clauses within a sentence, e.g. It was night but the moon was shining.
connective	a word or phrase that links clauses or sentences; can be conjunctions, e.g. while, when, because, therefore
consonant	a letter of the alphabet (e.g. p, t, m, b, x) that is not a vowel (a, e, i, o, u)
context	the time, place and events that relate to when a piece of text is written
dash	a punctuation mark used especially in informal writing to indicate a gap in time or a pause, e.g. The rest of the week was uneventful until – it happened again.
deduction	finding clues within a text that help develop understanding
definition	a brief precise statement of what a word or expression means, as in a dictionary or this glossary
dialect	the way English is spoken or written in different areas of the country
diminutive	a term that implies smallness. This may reflect a person's size or stature; or it may be used as a term of endearment, e.g. sweetie (to address a child or a loved one; Wills (for William)
exclamation mark	a punctuation mark used at the end of a sentence or an interjection to show strong emotion, e.g. What a shame!
font	a kind of typeface, e.g. Comic Sans, Times New Roman, which give a particular look to the words on a page
formal language	words that are written or spoken according to a set of rules
full stop	a punctuation mark used to mark the end of a sentence
grammar	the rules that apply to the relationships between words in any language
homonym	word that has the same spelling or pronunciation as another, but different meaning – may be a homograph, e.g. (dog) lead; lead (metal) or a homophone, e.g. hair, hare
hyphen	a punctuation mark that is sometimes used to join the two parts of a compound noun, as in golf-ball and proof-read
hypothesis	an explanation for the way something happens that is used as a basis for further investigation
idiom	an expression that is not meant literally, e.g. Pull your socks up and get on with it.
imagery	form of language used to create a vivid visual or sensory picture – alliteration, onomatopoeia, personification, simile and metaphor can all be used to do this
imperative verb	used for commands and instructions, e.g. Hold this!; Mix the ingredients together.
inference	to infer information that is not given directly but is implicit by reading around the content of a text
interjection	a sound, word, or phrase that expresses a strong emotion, such as pain or surprise, but otherwise has no meaning, e.g. Ow!
italics	printed or written letters that are deliberately made to slope to the right. Italics are used to emphasise words, e.g. You did *what*?
main clause	a clause which could stand alone as a sentence, e.g. There are no poisonous spiders in Britain, but many British people are scared of spiders.

3 Improve your skills: English essentials

metaphor	figure of speech used to describe somebody or something by comparison, e.g. lollipop trees
mnemonic	a short rhyme, phrase or other mental technique for making information easier to remember
noun: collective, proper, common, abstract	noun: a word or group of words used as the name of a class of people, places, or things, or of a specific person, place, or thing collective noun: used to describe a group of things, e.g. a flock of sheep proper noun: a place name or personal name, e.g. London; Mr Bean abstract noun: the name of an abstract idea, such as love or anger
onomatopoeia	the formation or use of words that imitate a sound, e.g. woof; miaow
opinion	a point of view
paragraph	a section of a piece of writing. A new paragraph indicates a change of focus, time or subject. It begins on a new line, usually with a one-line gap separating it from the previous paragraph
parenthesis	a word or phrase inserted into a sentence to explain or elaborate. It may be put in brackets or between dashes or commas
passive	where something or someone is having something done to them, e.g. Liz was pecked by the bird.
person: first, second, third	The first person is used in a piece of writing when a character is expressing their thoughts or speaking, e.g. My name is David and I will be 11 in June. The second person is used when addressing someone, e.g. Your name is David and you will be 11 in June. The third person is used when describing someone, e.g. His name is David and he will be 11 in June.
personification	giving human feelings, actions or characteristics to objects, e.g. The sun is smiling on us today; 'Wake up!' shouted the alarm clock.
phrase	a group of words that act as one unit. 'Dog' is a word, but 'the dog', 'a big dog' or 'that dog over there' are all phrases. Strictly speaking, a phrase can also consist of just one word, e.g. Boo!
plural	more than one
possessive apostrophe	when an apostrophe is used to show that something belongs to someone, e.g. Simon's peach
prefix	a group of letters that can be added to the beginning of a word to change its meaning, e.g. untidy
preposition	a word that indicates position, e.g. under, by, beside
pronoun: personal, possessive	a word that is used to replace a noun, e.g. 'She gave it to him', for 'Tilly gave the chocolate to Jack'. There are several kinds of pronouns. personal pronouns e.g. I/me, you, he/him, she/her, we/us, they/them, it possessive pronouns e.g. mine/yours, hers/his, ours/theirs
proverb	a saying that provides information about the world, or comments on it, e.g. Red sky at night, shepherds' delight.
pun	a play on words. A pun uses words that have similar sounds but different meanings to humorous effect, e.g. She trod on a grape and it let out a little wine.
punctuation	a way of marking text to help the reader's understanding
question mark	a punctuation mark used at the end of an interrogative sentence, e.g. Who are you?
rhetorical question	a question asked for effect that does not require an answer, e.g. Why me?

Glossary

rhyme	words that end with the same sound but not necessarily the same spelling
rhythm	he number of syllables used in each line to create a pattern of beats
root word	a word to which prefixes and suffixes can be added to make other words, e.g. tidy (untidy); telegraph (telegraphic)
scan	can mean two things: a) to look over a text very quickly, trying to locate information by locating a set words; or b) where a line of poetry conforms to the rhythm of the poem
semi-colon	a punctuation mark used to separate two main clauses in a sentence: I liked the book; it was about rugby, my favourite sport.
sentence	can be simple, compound or complex. A simple sentence consists of one clause, e.g. It rained. A compound sentence consists of two more clauses joined by 'and', 'but', or 'so', e.g. It was night so the lights were switched on. A complex sentence consists of more than one clause, e.g. The underground station, crowded with commuters, had an unusual smell and strange lights that flickered on and off.
simile	figure of speech that creates a picture by comparing one thing to another, e.g. as dead as a door nail. Many similes are idiomatic, e.g. He runs like a hare.
singular	form used to refer to one thing, animal or person, e.g. cat, monkey, parcel
skim	read quickly to get an initial overview of the subject matter and main ideas of a text
slang	words and phrases that are used in daily life and often linked with a particular region or used by people identifying with a particular group, e.g. 'That's wicked'
speech marks	inverted commas used to indicate where speech starts and ends, e.g. 'I've had a lot of fun today'
stage direction	an instruction for an actor or producer in the script of a play
subject	depending on the context: a word that performs the action expressed by the verb; a topic or theme, e.g. 'He gave me a strange look' and 'The cat hid under the sofa.'
subordinate clause	used with the main clause in a sentence which does not make sense on its own; it has a subject and a verb, but starts with a connective. A subordinate clause may come before, after or in the middle of a main clause
suffix	a group of letters that is added to the end of a word. There are two main categories: a) a suffix that changes the tense of a word from past to present, or from past to future; b) a suffix that changes the word from a verb to a noun, e.g. explore, explorer; or from a noun to an adjective, e.g. explorer, exploratory
superlative	describes the greatest, biggest, highest or most of something. The superlative form of an adjective or adverb typically has the ending '-est', e.g. the biggest fish in the river
syllable	Each beat in a word is a syllable. There are words with only one beat, e.g. hat, bright, sail; and words with more than one beat, e.g. hamper, picnic, hippopotamus.
synonym	a word with the same, or very similar, meaning as another word, e.g. dry, arid
tense	differing forms of a verb that reflect when actions take place: in the present, e.g. I am going; the past, e.g. I went; or in the future, e.g. I will go
verb	a word that shows what is happening or has happened, e.g. Emma feeds her goldfish twice a day; Luke ran across the field.
vowel	a letter of the alphabet that represents a vowel sound. In English, the vowels are a, e, i, o and u. Sometimes y is used like a vowel, e.g. synonym

4 Test for success

The next steps

Now you have completed your practice, you are ready to take the second set of more challenging Practice tests.

These Practice tests (located in the pull-out booklet) will confirm your ability to answer harder questions and highlight any areas that still need extra work.

Taking the second tests

Follow the guidance on page 10 for timing, equipment, surroundings, question types and tips then take the following tests in the order as outlined below.

Day 1

Reading test 2: 45 minutes

Dictation test 2: about 15 minutes.

Day 2

Writing task: 45 minutes each (select a 2* task in fiction if you chose a non-fiction task in Test 1; or a 2* task in non-fiction if you chose a fiction task in Test 1).

Spelling test 2: about 15 minutes.

Remember: this is a test to help you to find your strengths and weaknesses. Because of this it is important not to choose a multiple-choice option or guess randomly if you don't know the answer. In these instances it is better to leave the answer line blank.

Marking

Once you have completed the tests you will be ready to mark them. The process to follow is simple – the stages are listed below.

Reading test 2

- Turn to *Reading grid 2* on page 83 and complete this following the instructions on page 11.
- Transfer the total number of marks to the Summary box on page 85 and work out the percentage as directed.

Dictation test 2

- Go to *Dictation grid 2* on page 84 and complete this following the instructions on page 11.
- Transfer your final number to the Summary box on page 85. This is the percentage mark.

Writing task

- Go to *Writing grid* on page 15 if you have produced a fiction text or page 16 for a non-fiction text. Photocopy the grid so that you can use it again later. Follow the instructions on page 11 to complete the grid.
- Transfer your Levels for each section to the Summary boxes on page 85.

Spelling test 2

- Go to *Spelling grid 2* on page 84 and complete this following the instructions on page 11.
- Double the total to give your percentage and transfer this to the Summary box on page 85.

4 Test for success

Reading grid 2

Follow the instructions on page 11 to fill in this grid and page 13 for instructions for use.

Comprehension

Question	Mark*	Skill	Page	To do	Try it out	Test yourself
1		Skimming and scanning text	20			
2						
3		Finding information	22			
4						
5						
6						
7		Deduction and inference	26			
8						
9						
10		Organisation of text	28			
11						
12						
13						
14		How writers use language	30			
15						
16		Writer's viewpoint	32			
17						
18		Traditional and social context	34			
19						
Total	/19	Read 'Introducing comprehension' first on pages 18–19 if you have missed any Skills in the Comprehension section.				

Grammar

Question	Mark*	Skill	Page	To do	Try it out	Test yourself
20		Parts of speech	38			
21						
22						
23		Figurative language	40			
24						
25		Starting sentences	42			
26						
27		Agreement in sentences	44			
28						
29						
30						
Total	/11	Read 'Introducing grammar' first on pages 36–37 if you have missed any Skills in the Grammar section.				

Punctuation

Question	Mark*	Skill	Page	To do	Try it out	Test yourself
31		Basic punctuation	48			
32						
33						
34		More about punctuation	50			
35						
36						
Total	/6	Read 'Introducing punctuation' first on pages 46–47 if you have missed any Skills in the Punctuation section.				

Spelling

Question	Mark*	Skill	Page	To do	Try it out	Test yourself
37		Plurals and spelling rules	54			
38						
39		Doubling letters	56			
40						
41		Prefixes and suffixes	58			
42						
43		Tricky spellings	60			
44						
Total	/8	Read 'Introducing spelling' first on pages 52–53 if you have missed any Skills in the Spelling section.				

*1 mark is allocated for each correct answer. There are no half marks.

Total /44 Add up your total for your Reading test here.

4 Test for success

Dictation grid 2

Follow the instructions on page 11 to mark this grid.

It	was	late	.	There	were	shadows	on	the	wall	.	A	candle	stood	on	the	dining	table	,
its	light	reflected	in	the	mirror	hanging	over	the	fireplace	.	Photographs	were	arranged
on	the	window	ledge	with	a	plant	that	looked	rather	tired	.
"	When	is	Pete	getting	home	?	"	asked	Hannah	,	looking	at	the	clock	.
"	I	'm	not	sure	,	"	replied	her	Mum	,	trying	to	sound	calm	and	unconcerned	.
First	there	had	been	the	sound	of	an	explosion	and	then	the	power	cut	.
Could	it	all	be	linked	?

The Dictation test can help you to identify problems in your own creative writing. If there are a lot of errors, you may find that you often think of a word but leave it out because you have difficulty in writing it down.

Look carefully at the errors in your test and see if you have left words out, missed punctuation marks or put in additional words.

The test will also give you practice in proof-reading your own work and help you to improve this.

If you miss punctuation, this could highlight a problem with your understanding of sentence structure. Revising parts of speech and sentence construction (see pages 38–39 and 42–45) will help to improve this.

Spelling grid 2

Follow the instructions on page 11 to mark this grid.

A	bit	cat	get	lot	put	
	the	one	was	are	they	
B	this	chin	most	left	band	
	said	four	who	again	next	
C	tape	chair	house	share	east	
	light	could	until	enough	many	
D	people	before	settle	limit	size	
	laugh	quiet	comb	truly	written	
E	disappear	business	introduction	medicine	vehicle	
	choir	orchestra	necessary	parliament	advertisement	
					Total	

Look carefully at the types of word you have spelt incorrectly in the test. If you found a lot of errors in parts A and B of the test, you may benefit from revising your phonics. Make sure you check internal vowels as well as the beginning and ending letters or blends.

If you found a lot of errors in parts C and D you would benefit from revising the Spelling section of this book (see pages 52–61).

If you had difficulty with the second lines of each part and found part E challenging, it is time to practise the exercises in the Spelling sections to find ways to help you get these irregular word spellings into your long-term memory.

4 Test for success

Now that you have all your results from the second set of Practice tests you can celebrate your success in areas where you have improved and plan for your final preparations.

Reviewing the final summary boxes

Look at your results in the Summary boxes below and review your scores. To be prepared for the 11+ tests you should be aiming to achieve results of 80% or higher in Reading and Dictation and results of 70% or higher in Writing and Spelling.

If you still have areas that need additional practice you can…

- revisit the relevant pages in the guide
- purchase additional materials linked to the specific skills you have identified in these tests.

If you are now achieving the suggested percentages, you should move on to take some 11+ Practice papers to boost your confidence and further develop your familiarity with the different question types you may encounter. These tests are also useful for increasing your speed in answering the questions.

Practice support

You may find the following Letts titles helpful for additional skills practice…

- English Ages 9–10 Assessment Papers Levels 3–5   9781844192212
- English Ages 10–11 Assessment Papers Levels 4–5   9781844192229
- More English Ages 10–11 Years Assessment Papers Levels 4–5   9781844195534

You may find the following Letts Practice papers helpful for your final preparations…

- 11+ Practice Papers Multiple Choice English   9781844192519

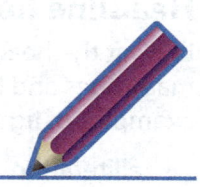

Summary boxes

Reading test 2
Total ☐
Percentage ☐
Work out your percentage using this sum
$\frac{\text{Total}}{44} \times 100 =$

Dictation test 2
Total ☐
Percentage ☐

Writing task 2
Section | Level
Grammar ☐
Punctuation ☐
Spelling ☐
Text structure ☐

Spelling test 2
Total ☐
Percentage ☐
Work out your percentage using this sum
$\frac{\text{Total}}{50} \times 100 =$

5 Show what you can do

Try following the steps given here to break your time down into easy-to-manage stages. This will help you feel much more in control and relaxed about your preparation.

Playing games in the weeks leading up to the tests helps you to become familiar with the skills you will need. You can share your preparation with your parents.

Reading games
Street scanner
Play this game when you're on a walk or in the car. It will help you to find a range of different words with the same or similar meaning, to prevent your writing becoming boring or to help you scan for information within a text.

- How many different words can you find that name a road?
  Examples: Road, Street, Lane.

Secret seals
Go through the post with your parents. Guess what type of letter it is and who it might be from by looking at various clues:

- Where is the postmark from?
- Is it handwritten or typed?
- Is it franked or does it have a stamp?
  Examples: Bank statement, advertisement, personal letter.

Headline horrors
Look at the headlines in newspapers and magazines and look for the following examples of figurative language:

- alliteration
- metaphors and similes
- onomatopoeia.
  Examples: Dangerous Doctor Dupes Public!; Council Adopts Lollipop Lamposts; Daft as a Brush!

Punk-tuation
Go through a text and highlight the punctuation marks using a different bright colour for each type of mark:

- commas, colons, semi-colons, ellipses.
  For example: The rabbit, with green fur, rushed into the room and shouted "Fire!"

  You may be surprised what you have missed out. Ask an adult to check it.

Writing tips
There are quick ways to help you remember ways to vary your sentences.

The 'Rule of five': Have you started a sentence with a verb, a noun, an adverb, an adjective and a preposition?

Simple activities can develop skills in writing:

- write a holiday diary
- be imaginative with notes on the fridge.

TRY IT OUT
Silly rhymes
If there is something you really can't remember, make up a silly phrase or rhyme. For difficult spellings use the initial letters to make up a sentence, for example:

- Metaphor: Mum made mountainous mulberry muffins.
- Richard Hit Your Tambourine Hard Mark: RHYTHM

5 Show what you can do

Preparing for the 11+ tests

Countdown to the tests

As soon as possible before the tests...

Check with the school you are applying to about their entrance requirements:

- Find out what exams your chosen school will be setting.
- Make sure you know the dates.

One week before the tests

- Check your travel arrangements and practise getting to the destination to make sure you know where to go.
- Make sure you have enough pens, pencils and an analogue watch so you can see how much time you have spent if you are timing your work.
- If you are taking a Maths paper as well as English, check with the school if you need geometry equipment (ruler, set squares, protractor, compasses) and whether you can bring tracing paper and a mirror. Any equipment will need to be taken in a see-through pencil case.

During the week before the tests

- Allow yourself 90 minutes to check through any areas you're worried about up to two days before.
- Avoid last minute practice as this can make you anxious – do something with your friends or parents to help you relax the night before.
- Get a good night's sleep.

The day of the tests

- Eat a good breakfast.
- Leave in plenty of time, making allowances for traffic and other hold-ups.
- Take a healthy snack to boost your energy levels and a small bottle of water.
- Go to the toilet before you go in to the test.

During the tests

- Read the questions twice before you start writing.
- Make sure you understand what you are expected to do. For example, make sure you know how many selections you are being asked to make in multiple-choice questions and how you are supposed to mark down your answer.
- Underline key words in the questions.
- Make sure you know which questions get most marks. Spend your time accordingly.
- After half the time is up, check whether you have got to the stapled pages in the test. If you haven't, go through and do the easy questions in the second half of the paper.
- Even if you are in a hurry, make sure your work is easy to read.
- If you can't do a question, leave it. Come back to it at the end if you have time.
- Leave time at the end to check your work.

English papers

- In papers with 'written format' questions some responses will ask for single-word answers, others for full sentences. Make sure you know which are which. You are only likely to encounter these question types if your local authority, school or an examination board has written their own papers.
- Plan your work in writing tasks, even if you only put your ideas down as single words and phrases.
- If you are writing a story and you're running out of time, make notes of how your story will finish as this will give you some marks for finishing.

Interview techniques

5 Show what you can do

Many schools base their final selection on how well the applicants perform in an interview.

With the right preparation, you can use this opportunity to show your potential to be a good member of the school and find out whether this is the right place for you.

Discussion topics

Being prepared with interesting things to talk about during your interview is always a good idea.

If you have recently visited a museum, National Trust or English Heritage property these make ideal subjects to prepare for discussion. If you have taken part in a sporting event such as a rugby tournament or a cross-country run, these make equally good talking points.

Rather than writing down lots of information, take a small business card and create a spider diagram on the back. This diagram will remind you of the key points of interest that you can talk about, given the right opportunity by the interviewer.

Who would enjoy visiting this museum?
I think that this museum would appeal to…because…

Where?
Recently I visited…It was interesting because…

Cost?
I think that this trip was/wasn't very good value for money as…

Museum

What was really good about the visit?
I really enjoyed… as I learnt about…

What do you think could be improved at the museum?
It was a pity that…I think this could be improved by…

What was the best display?
I think the best display in the museum…was…because

Meeting the interviewer

Waiting

- Calm yourself with the breathing techniques shown in the box, opposite.
- Do talk to other candidates who are waiting, but don't pester them for information.
- Read useful information on posters and notice boards in the room.

Entering the interview room

- Knock before you enter.
- Say 'hello' in a friendly and polite way.
- Shake hands firmly if the interviewer offers their hand.
- Wait for the interviewer to indicate a seat before you sit down.

RELAX

These techniques can help to calm your nerves when you are waiting to go into the interview room.

- Imagine you are holding an eggshell in each hand. This helps to relax your fingers and release tension.
- Breathe in slowly through your nose, counting to three and breathe out at the same pace. Concentrate on your breathing to clear your mind.

5 Show what you can do

Interview techniques

Body language

Basic body language
- Sit in a relaxed way, but don't slouch.
- Sit so that your body, including your legs and feet, points towards the interviewer.
- Don't put up barriers by crossing your arms in front of you.
- Smile, but only when appropriate – don't just grin all the time.

Hands
- Keep your hands away from your face and hair.
- Don't touch your nose before you answer a question.
- Use your hands to express yourself, but keep them on your lap at other times.

Eye contact
- Look at the interviewer, but don't stare – remember to blink.
- Don't be tempted to look away if they ask a difficult question.
- Don't shut your eyes while you think about a question.

Asking and answering questions

Avoiding yes/no answers
- Every question is an opportunity to tell the interviewer something about yourself.
- Don't just answer 'Yes' or 'No'. Give *positive* answers.
- Try adding an example to your answer, or qualify it ('No, but …', 'Yes, although I sometimes …').

Difficult questions
- If you're asked about an area of weakness, explain how you've tried to improve.
- If you're asked a factual question and don't know the answer, say so.
- If you don't understand a question, ask for it to be repeated or ask for an explanation.

Asking questions
- Prepare your own questions in advance.
- Don't ask questions you could easily find out the answers to.
- Ask a question that shows you have done some research about the school and would like to find out more.

Ending the interview

Thanking the interviewer
- Thank the interviewer for their time.
- Add something like, 'I've enjoyed talking with you.'

Saying goodbye
- Respond with a firm handshake if the interviewer offers their hand.
- Close the door quietly when you leave.

DRESS

First impressions are important. Find out in advance about what you should wear. Your current school uniform is usually a suitable option.

- Make sure that the clothes you are wearing are clean and ironed and that your shoes are clean.
- Make sure your hair is tidy and that your fringe isn't too long so that your eyes can be seen. If your hair is long, tie it back.

QUESTIONS

Think about questions you could ask at the end of your interview. They could be questions about the school in general or about specific subjects or sports that interest you. Here are some examples:

- What is special about your secondary school that is different from the other schools in the area?
- What are the most popular universities students choose when leaving the school?
- I really enjoy rugby. Are there opportunities to take part in inter-school competitions?

5 Show what you can do

After the tests

Once you have taken the tests, the marking and admissions process begins.

Although you'll need to wait to hear if you have been given a place at the school, you can spend some of the time finding out about what happens next.

Waiting for results

Results for the 11+ tests do not come quickly and you should expect to wait between 10 and 16 weeks. If the school you have applied to has not already told you when the results will be available, ask a parent to check the date with the school or the Local Education Authority (LEA).

Understanding the results

The pass mark

The pass mark can change from year to year as it is based on how many places there are at the school. You may also find that the pass mark for boys and girls is different – this happens when a school wants to balance the number of students from each sex in the year group.

Standardisation

In order to make the testing process fair, scores are *standardised* by age. This means that if you are one of the younger children in your age group, the school will take this into account when deciding your final marks.

When the results are not as you expect

Offers from LEA schools

If you have applied to an LEA school, you will have been offered a choice of up to three schools.

If you don't get into your first choice of school, your name will be placed on the list for your second choice. Although the schools generally take students who have put them down first on the list, there are sometimes a few spare places. If your second choice of school is full then you will be passed on to your third choice, so don't give up hope!

Offers from private and independent schools

If you have applied to a private or independent school you will not be offered an alternative school unless you have applied to these separately and taken their 11+ tests as well.

What to do if you don't agree with the result

If you haven't been lucky enough to get a place at your chosen school, your family have a right to find out why. It may be that your test results were the reason for being turned down but there could also be other reasons such as the distance you live from the school.

When you have found out the reasons but you're not happy with what you have been told, your family can put in an 'appeal' (if it is a local authority school) to see if you can get the decision changed.

Although appeals are usually carried out in a friendly way, the process is quite formal. There are a number of organisations that can help with advice, including the Advisory Centre for Education (ACE). There is also a wide selection of private companies who specialise in supporting families in putting appeals forward.

Test answers

Comprehension

Skimming and scanning — 20

1. C: 'Car thief foiled by games girls' – this captures most about the story.
2. No. '… members of the public should not aim to harm criminals.'

Finding information (1) — 22

1. D: Seven people were in the boat: 'the seven-person crew…'
2. B: The boat was going to Hawaii: 'our goal of making it to Hawaii.'
3. The Polynesians went to Hawaii 'more than a thousand years ago.'

Finding information (2) — 24

1. C: The baby is wearing a nappy: 'its nappy forming a solid base.'
2. D: Dom doesn't like being with the baby – he says he is having a 'lovely' time, but that's a lie. This is shown in the last paragraph where he holds the toys out of reach.
3. Dom is not nice – he is mean to the baby, he taunts it with the bricks and tries to make it topple over. He smiles when the baby cries (the answer must be explained to gain the mark).

Deduction and inference — 26

1. From the words the writer uses when describing what the wolf is thinking.

    Clues: gobble

    Related words to eat: dessert

    Emotive language: succulent
2. C: Leather trousers: 'her leather-clad leg'.

Organisation of text — 28

1. The first paragraph gives a brief summary of the episode and its mystery. It tells us what the article is about and draws us in to read the rest of it. The next paragraph gives more information and makes it more mysterious. The third and fourth paragraphs give authority to the mystery – neither the spokesman nor the scientists can explain it. The last paragraph also extends the mystery, making it more intriguing.
2. D: Scientists can't explain the 'rain of birds'.

How writers use language — 30

1. By using 'your', the writer tries make you feel you have already chosen Adrian. If you think of him as 'your' rep, you will vote for him.
2. D: The writer suggests you would be foolish not to vote for Adrian – you would be deliberately doing something that is not sensible, and that you know is not sensible. This makes you more likely to vote for him.

Writer's viewpoint — 32

1. No, the writer thinks children should be allowed to wear whatever they like.
2. B: Children in uniform are stifled and their individuality suffocated.

Traditional and social context — 34

1. The first line is 'Once upon a time' which is often the start of a fairy story.
2. The beautiful girl, the poor family, the house in a village, the forest, the blood-red rose and the dark tower are all common features in fairy tales.
3. Because the tower is dark, behind a high wall and has a locked gate, it is likely that a bad person lives there.
4. It will probably have a happy ending, and most fairy tales do.

Improve your skills answers

Test answers

Grammar

Parts of speech — 38

1. Alice was beginning to get very tired of sitting by her sister on the bank and of having nothing to do: once or twice she had peeped into the book her sister was reading, but it had no pictures or conversations in it "and what is the use of a book," thought Alice, "without pictures or conversations?"

2. 'twice' is an adverb as it describes when Alice did something – she 'peeped' (verb) into the book 'once or twice'.

Figurative language — 40

1. 'A snake of rope slithering across the deck' is a metaphor – it means the rope looks and moves like a snake. It helps us imagine the slow, stealthy movement of the rope and the idea of a snake makes it rather sinister and threatening.

2. C: The 'flag flapped lazily' uses alliteration as it repeats the same sound at the start of words.

Starting sentences — 42

1. C: 'Trekking through forest…' starts with a verb.

2. The first sentence starts with a noun, 'leeches'. It is an exciting start to the article that draws you in. The scene is unusual and 'leeches' is an unusual word with which to start a sentence, so it makes you want keep reading.

Agreement in sentences — 44

1. Hannah and Alice <u>was</u> going to the shops. It <u>is</u> Saturday, so they could stay out all day – there was no school. Alice <u>wants</u> to buy some blue tights, and Hannah wanted to buy green socks. The first shop they <u>go</u> to <u>were</u> closed because it <u>were</u> being redecorated. The next shop <u>is</u> large and the girls could not find tights and socks, so they <u>ask</u> an assistant. 'Socks and tights, and every other type of accessory, <u>is</u> on the ground floor,' she <u>says</u>.

   Hannah and Alice **were** going to the shops. It **was** Saturday, so they could stay out all day – there was no school. Alice **wanted** to buy some blue tights, and Hannah wanted to buy green socks. The first shop they **went** to **was** closed because it **was** being redecorated. The next shop **was** large and the girls could not find tights and socks, so they **asked** an assistant. 'Sock and tights, and every other type of accessory, **are** on the ground floor,' she **said**.

   The one you are most likely to have missed is 'Socks and tights, and every other type of accessory, **are** on' – the subject is 'socks and tights', so it's plural.

2. D: 'Adrian and Bernard want to go to the cinema' is the only one that agrees properly.

92

Test answers

Punctuation

Basic punctuation — 48

1 Gabrielle closed the door and sat on the bed. It was gloomy, but she was sure she saw something out of the corner of her eye. Could there be someone in the room? She didn't want to turn the light on – just in case there was. She tried to calm her nerves. But she had only been there a minute when she heard something rustle softly. There was someone – or something – there. What was it she heard? It wasn't quite rustling. It was more muffled. It entered her head that it was a noise of feathers. A bird!

A bird must have got trapped in her room! She sighed with relief and turned on the light. There was no bird. Beside the wardrobe stood – could it be? Yes, unbelievably – an angel!

2 B: 'It was yellow and very smelly.'

This has a capital letter at the start, a full stop at the end and contains a subject and a verb.

More about punctuation — 50

1 We packed some snacks to take in the boat: sandwiches, apples, cakes, lemonade and crisps. Hattie wanted to take bananas, but I said they'd get squashed. She grumbled and started to sulk. "Shut up!" Dan said. Hattie started to cry; the trip was going wrong already. "Here, Hattie," I said, "why don't you find a picnic blanket? And some sweets; they won't get squashed."

2 C: This is correctly punctuated. 'A' is inconsistent, using first a comma and then a semi-colon to separate the list items. A semi-colon is best as each item is a phrase. 'B' links two unconnected main phrases with a comma. It should be two sentences, or a sentence split with a semi-colon. 'D' is inconsistent as it uses a dash to start the bit in parenthesis and a comma to end it; dashes would be best.

Improve your skills answers

Test answers

Spelling

Plurals and spelling rules 54

1 C: 'Potatoes' is the only one that is spelt correctly; the others should be 'mosquitoes', 'eyelashes', 'matches' and 'monkeys'.

2 Brigit would have liked camping better if there had not been so many mosquitoes. They bit her arms and legs and even her eye lids, near her lashes. She liked everything else – cooking potatoes in the embers of the camp fire, toasting marshmallows and flicking matches into the fire – but the best thing of all was watching the monkeys swing in the trees.

Doubling letters 56

1 Hoping; enjoying; wanting; asking; following; having; doing; endangering.

2 D: this answer is wrongly spelt; it should be 'feeling'. As there is double 'e' before the 'l', you don't need to double the letter.

Prefixes and suffixes 58

1 You can make these words by adding prefixes: bi*cycle*, un*interesting*, un*happy*, anti*clockwise*, dis*comfort*, non-*fiction*, super*market*.

2 B: this answer has a spelling mistake: faithfuly should be spelt faithfully – the 'l' must be doubled because the suffix is 'ly' and 'faithful' ends with 'l'.

Tricky words 60

1 Our science field trip to the pond was very hare-raising. We sore lots of minibeasts in the water, but that's knot all that happened. Pedro rode across the pond in a boat, but he took the wrong root and got stuck in the reads. The son was very bright, and he was stuck four too ours before Mr Williams noticed and through a rope to him. He tide the rope to a peace of would at the front of the boat and Mr Williams helped pull him to the sure. Annabelle was stung by a be, and Katie was throne in the water by some bad buoys. We aren't aloud to go on any moor school trips in the currant year.

The correct words are: hair, saw, not, rowed, route, reeds, sun, for, two, hours, threw, tied, piece, wood, shore, bee, thrown, boys, allowed, more, current.

2 D: 'sandwidge' should be spelled 'sandwich'.

Reading test 1 *answers*

1. An answer that explains that it was the last squirrel in the country/world.
2. E: chaotic
3. A type of newspaper.
4. B: 2 and 4 only
5. Accept any of the following: There were no birds singing/few wild animals/more pollution.
6. E: trees
7. An answer that shows Amy is very interested or very excited.
8. D: she was impatient to see the squirrel
9. D: computer-generated tree
10. An answer that explains that bold type makes words stand out from the rest of the text/shows that it is from a newspaper.
11. D: at an underground station
12. An answer that explains that a word in italics shows that Amy is very keen to go to see the squirrel.
13. D: a flashback in time
14. Accept either of the following: An answer that explains that something terrible had happened/ The writer wants to emphasise how awful it was.
15. D: They show that she is interested.
16. An answer that quotes or states that squirrels were 'enchanting little creatures with feathered, furry tails.'
17. E: menacing, airless, packed
18. Any answer that backs a viewpoint with examples from the text, e.g.:
    No, because there wouldn't be any birds.
    Yes, because I would like to find out about the machines.
19. C: in the future
20. E: adjective
21. A: noun
22. C: sadder, quieter
23. B: metaphor ('feathered, furry')
24. A: The click, click
25. E: hunched
26. D: reversed
27. B: will carry
28. E: were
29. C: had been
30. E: taken
31. B: built in 2020, was below
32. The trains, which dated from before the dreadful accident, had torn seats, rusty window frames, chewing gum covered floors and a strange metallic smell.
33. Amy, Pete, Jenny and Himal had read about squirrels, small tree-dwelling rodents, in their school natural history books.
34. B: loved hazelnuts; they *or* loved hazelnuts. They
35. "Please can we take mum next time?" pleaded Amy.
36. Dad looked thoughtful, "Do you think the trains will be this crowded all day?" he asked.
37. A: there used to be **monkeys**
38. The **cities** were growing bigger with more **people**, more **children** and more animals everywhere; even in the **parks**.
39. D: better
40. Amy thought that the squirrel looked **distressed** as it **hopped** and **skipped** around the strange **artificial** tree.
41. C: that were ringing
42. The carriage was **un**tidy with litter, careless**ly** strewn under the bench seats, which were in a state of **dis**repair.
43. C: committee
44. The **menacing** machines towered over the **station**, their ominous **fluorescent** lights flashing **messages**.

Test answers

Reading test 2 answers

1. Iceland and Greenland
2. D: Baltic Sea
3. B: weather
4. C: They didn't try to spread their religion.
5. D: 3 and 4 only
6. Plutarch
7. An answer that shows that the Vikings attacked the churches and monasteries, so that the priests and monks who wrote the records would be anti-Viking.
8. E: 982 AD
9. B: Priests were the main group of people that could read and write.
10. An answer that explains that each question is a heading for a paragraph, and that each paragraph goes on to answer the question. Any answer that shows an understanding of the text structure is acceptable.
11. C: What we know about the Vikings
12. An answer that explains the italics are used to indicate key words and that bold typeface is used for headings.
13. D: Friend or foe?
14. C: products
15. 'Chronicles' suggest that they were chronological records, logs or diaries and were an accurate record of events.
16. Farming communities
17. A: They brought valuable articles to trade.
18. The work of the historian Plutarch and the Oseberg tapestry.
19. E: in an encyclopedia
20. B: noun
21. D: preposition
22. E: verb
23. B: alliteration
24. D: simile
25. C: Negotiation
26. A: Typical
27. *build; cross; loot; return*
28. *provided; understanding; would have; ruled*
29. C: were, changed
30. D: does, are
31. A: Their swift wooden longships,
32. The brother and sister Frey and Freyja, the god and goddess of fertility, were also important and there were many other minor gods and goddesses.
33. Viking children had wooden dolls, played football, sailed model boats and played horn trumpets.
34. C: "more like greedy plunderers
35. C: Vikings: they weren't *or* Vikings; they weren't *or* Vikings – they weren't
36. King Alfred, pray to your god and wait to see what happens, because the Viking Guthrun's coming with all his mates.
37. A: I showed off all my jewellery,
38. **Wolves**, bears and **sheep** were the animals we knew best in our home **countries**.
39. C: terrible, dribbling, dagger
40. The Saxon farmer was **splitting** logs and **stripping** the bark from the strong young **saplings**.
41. The Saxons were **re**arranging and clear**ing** their village longhouse after the **un**expect**ed** raid by the Vikings.
42. The Saxons were **dis**organised and **un**prepared for the sudden raid on the **un**protected coastline.
43. D: allowed, their
44. The Vikings loved to **practise** their rowing skills and sang **mischievous** songs about their **friends** and **enemies**.